The Complete Guide To

RESTORING &

MAINTAINING

WOOD

FURNITURE

& CABINETS

The Complete Guide To

RESTORING &
MAINTAINING
WOOD
FURNITURE
& CABINETS

B R A D   H U G H E S

BETTERWAY BOOKS

Cincinnati, Ohio

Photographs in color insert by Geoffrey Kilmer

Text photographs by Brad Hughes

Page layout by Studio 500

Typography by Blackhawk Typesetting

The Complete Guide to Restoring and Maintaining Wood Furniture and Cabinets.
Copyright © 1993 by Brad Hughes. Printed and bound in the United States of America. All
rights reserved. No part of this book may be reproduced in any form or by any electronic or
mechanical means including information storage and retrieval systems without permission
in writing from the publisher, except by a reviewer, who may quote brief passages in a review.
Published by Betterway Books, an imprint of F&W Publications, Inc., 1507 Dana Avenue,
Cincinnati, Ohio 45207. 1-800-289-0963. First edition.

97 96 95 94 93   5 4 3 2 1

Library of Congress Cataloging-in-Publication Data

Hughes, Brad.
    The complete guide to restoring and maintaining wood furniture and cabinets
/ Brad Hughes.
        p. cm.
    Includes index.
    ISBN 1-55870-302-0
1. Furniture finishing. 2. Furniture—Repairing. I. Title.
TT199.4.H83 1993
684.1'044—dc20   93-24796
                                                                            CIP

To my best friend, my wife

Bett

Acknowledgments

My sincerest thanks to Patrick O'Rourke, whose help, dedication, and friendship have been a great asset in completing this project. I look forward to working with him in the future, and wish all the best to Patrick.

Thanks to Lori Alexander, for the sketch work and the many hours dedicated to this project.

I also wish to thank my friend Geoffrey Kilmer at Photoworks for the time he worked in his studio on photographs. A grateful thank-you to Hugh Wilson, who motivated me to get to work and complete the book.

Finally, to Ashley Carter, my pen pal, friend, shining star, and little niece in New York, I love you.

Foreword

The cost of a piece of furniture and its value are often two very different matters. An object's cost is simply the price that was paid for purchasing the object — a clear, definite monetary amount, barter agreement, or trade. An object's value can be highly subjective. Is it an exceptional or unusual example of its kind? Was it made by a renowned cabinet-maker or artist? Is it a family heirloom? Was it once owned by a famous person? Does it have a clear chain of ownership from the time it was made until now? Does the owner, for whatever reason, have a special fondness for it? Value, like beauty, often lies in the eye of the beholder.

However the furniture owner derives the value of an object, with that value comes a responsibility. If the object has value now, the owner is responsible for maintaining the object in such a way that its value will not be diminished by lack of care or by intrusive cleaning or refinishing techniques. In a sense, we never really own the objects that have value for us. Our role can best be defined as that of caretaker — we are stewards of those objects in our possession, inheriting them from the stewards of the past and preserving them for the next generations.

It has been a joy to see Brad Hughes approach furniture projects with just this sensitivity. Brad evaluates an object as though he were a detective. He seeks to discover the activities involved in originally creating the object, then to learn what practices and changes the object has undergone. Only after answering these questions does he then propose a treatment plan, which almost always involves the gentlest methods possible to improve the object's appearance.

This book reflects Brad's expertise, as well as his sense of humor, as he guides the furniture owner through the maze of finishes, cleaning and care techniques, and restoration options. He also tells of his past successes (and even a few failures) that have made him the professional he is today.

Something tells me that Brad had as much fun writing this book as you will reading it.

James E. Wootton
Curator, Ash Lawn-Highland
Home of President James Monroe

Contents

Introduction

I began this project with this thought in mind: What would have been most helpful to me twenty-two years ago, when I began working on furniture? What I have learned is what I wish to pass on to you. This book is written for those who wish to care for their furniture and cabinets and/or to refinish furniture and avoid many of the problems I encountered in the past. This book is not written for the professional restorer but will be helpful as I detail caring for or restoring the furniture in your home.

In 1971 I was home from the Army and working on my first refinishing project in the spare bedroom. What a mess it was, as I sanded that old pie safe and filled the place with dust. The only way I knew to remove the paint and old finish was by sanding, so I went after it with my orbital sander. I suppose if the old pie safe could have spoken, it would have screamed for mercy. But somehow I did remove the old paint and finish, refinished the piece, and put it in my living room. My friends would comment on how good the pie safe looked. As a result, it wasn't long before the whole house was furnished with different pieces I had bought at yard sales or flea markets. Ten dollars for this or twenty for that, and I had collected and refinished a house full of furniture.

I enjoyed working on furniture and learning the age, characteristics, and background of different pieces I saw in the furniture books I collected and read, and of the pieces I had in my home. I clearly remember looking at many old pieces and thinking how good I could make them look by working my refinishing "magic." The thought never crossed my mind that many of the finishes I was stripping could be restored and given new life.

I began to learn more when I started refinishing kitchen cabinet doors. These doors often had a soft, dark finish around the pulls, caused by the particular area being touched so frequently. I would refinish the doors and drawers and then touch up the case and give it a new coat of finish to match the doors. I was beginning to learn what caused old finishes to discolor and deteriorate, what could be done to prevent this and, most important, that old finishes could be given new life.

The knowledge I gained has been the result of working on furniture for twenty-two years. My many friends in the furniture business have always been willing to take the time to answer the many questions I have asked. I believe you can have lots of fun working on the furniture in your home and get the same pride and satisfaction I have over the years, seeing pieces come to life again.

Protecting the value, adding value to your furniture and cabinets, saving money, and finally, completing a project you can be proud of — these are what I hope you will achieve as you read this book.

Part I

Maintaining Your Furniture

1.
The Finish

If you picked up this book and read only the first paragraph, what would be the most important thing I would like you to read and, hopefully, to remember? The number one, most important thing is this: *if you are cleaning and waxing your furniture and cabinets with the wrong products, you will be harming the finish.* There, I've given it my best shot, and I hope you will remember it and check what is happening to the wood in your home. If you read no further, I hope you will at least call someone who has experience with furniture and get him or her to recommend products for you to use.

When I was eleven years old, back in 1961, my grandfather gave me an old single barrel 12-gauge shotgun. I was just old enough to start hunting for squirrels and will never forget how proud I was of that gun. After every hunting trip and many times in between, I would clean and polish my old shotgun. Since my gun never looked as good as I thought it should, I somehow got the notion that I could refinish the stock and make it look much better. It wasn't long before I made a trip to the hardware store and purchased the supplies I needed for my very first refinishing project.

In hindsight, almost everything I did to refinish my gun was wrong. When I was eleven I didn't know a whole heck of a lot about refinishing. I just knew I wanted my gun stock to look better than it did. Somehow, I did make the old gun look much better.

Over thirty years have passed, and I have refinished or repaired several thousand pieces of furniture. There seems to be a never-ending variety of pieces to work on, and there is always a challenge waiting.

MY EXPERIENCE WITH CABINETS

When I first began refinishing furniture as a business, I was called to refinish a set of kitchen cabinets. The customer complained that the area around the pulls on her cabinets had become dark and soft. She was shocked that when she cleaned the soft area the finish came off, exposing the bare wood.

I had seen the same type of damage to the finish on chair arms and chair backs. The complaint was the same: the finish would become soft and dark, and when cleaned off the bare wood would be exposed.

It wasn't long before I learned that there was a good market for refinishing kitchen cabinet doors to match their original color. This was a real savings to the customer, as refinishing the whole set of cabinets would usually cost three times as much. Doing a complete refinishing job also meant stripping cabinets in the customer's home and creating quite a mess for at least a week or two. To refinish just the cabinet doors, I could go into a kitchen, take the cabinet doors down and remove the drawers in forty-five minutes, and take them to my shop to do all the dirty work. In a week I would return and rehang refinished doors and drawers that looked at least as good as new. As a final touch, I would go over the body of the cabinets and touch up any nicks or scratches and work on any area of the finish that didn't look as good as it should.

This was good work and good experience for me. It helped me to learn many things about problems with cabinet and furniture finishes. I saw that many of the same problems with finishes occurred in kitchens that appeared to be immaculate, as opposed to those that were not quite as clean. Three areas were typically the problem areas on many cabinets that I worked on. These were the area below the sink, the area above the range, and the area around the pulls on the drawers and doors. If I were being called about a problem with the finish on a set of cabinets, surely one, if not all, of these areas was a problem.

Finishing Doors and Drawers

I gained a lot of experience working on kitchen cabinet finishes. When a customer called to inquire about refinishing his cabinets, one of the first questions I asked was: "Are you happy with the color of your cabinets now?" If the customer said yes, I knew without seeing the cabinets that in most cases I could refinish the doors to match and would offer this as a possible option to the customer. My customers were always interested in this option when I explained how much money, mess, and inconvenience could be saved by refinishing the doors rather than the entire cabinets.

PREVENTING THE NEED FOR REFINISHING

I have gone into this long explanation at this point for only one reason. *If the finish had been kept clean on these cabinet doors in the first place, they would not have needed refinishing.* Waxing the finish is important, but keeping the finish clean is even more important. The way you care for your furniture and the products you use to do this will make an enormous difference in how your furniture will look and how long the finish will last. Whatever you put on the finish or fail to remove from it will preserve or damage it.

To put first things first, we should take a close look at the finish on your furniture or cabinets. Then we will begin to understand some of the factors that cause problems to the various kinds of finishes. The following is a brief history of the furniture finish and an outline of the ways a finish can be harmed.

TYPES OF FINISHES

You will hear about many different finishes that can be used on your furniture or cabinets. Some of these are polyurethane, varnish, tung oil, shellac, and lacquer. There are others, too, but the two main workhorse finishes of the furniture industry over the last two hundred years are shellac and lacquer. It wasn't until I began to repair damaged furniture finishes that I understood why these were the most widely used for furniture.

The finish on wood is designed to do two things: enhance the beauty of the wood and provide a protective coating. Many finishes do a good job of enhancing the beauty of the wood, but the major differences become obvious in their levels of durability as protective coating.

Early Finishes

Let's go back to the days when James Monroe was President. We will walk into his dining room and look at the table where he would have eaten. If it were his first term in office (1817-21), the finish on the table would have been wax or possibly one of many different types of varnish finishes that varnish peddlers sold from shop to shop. It's impossible to determine exactly what materials these finishes would have contained. General types of materials listed in cabinetmaker's recipe books from that era include waxes, most often beeswax; gums, such as rosin, gum mastic, and dammer; and oils, including linseed and poppyseed oils. Color was most often added to the finish rather than to the wood. Pigments such as dragon's blood, indigo (both plant derivatives), and verdigris were common, and essentially the same colorants used in the textile industry were used for furniture finishes. Then these ingredients would be combined in some proportion, but there was little consistency or quality control of the available varnishes.

Shellac

As President Monroe entered his golden years, a new finish had just begun to be used in France that

This dining table was used by James Monroe in his administration in the White House.
It is an early example of a shellac finish.

would become the most popular finish used by the furniture industry for the next 125 years. What was this shiny new finish everyone liked so much in France? The new finish was shellac. Unlike other finishes, it was very fast drying. Shellac was destined to become the craze in the United States very soon. Many of the wax finishes used by American furniture makers were thus stripped off and the new shellac finish applied. It was certainly the fashionable thing to do at the beginning of the nineteenth century.

Let's take at look at why shellac caught on so fast and became the mainstay of the furniture industry for so long.

European interest in the use of shellac originated in the early seventeenth century, as lacquered works from China and Japan were imported into Italy and were dispersed from there throughout Europe. The use of shellac as a furniture finish did not become fashionable until the late eighteenth century, however. (In the intervening years, *japanning* was the finish of choice. Japanning is discussed below.)

In Colonial times, many pieces were finished with wax or varnishes that were peddled from shop to shop. In the early nineteenth century, it became popular to strip these pieces and apply shellac.

Shellac is produced in Indochina and India from the secretions of the female *Laccifer lacca* beetle. The beetle can only produce lac from certain trees, the best known being the banyan tree. The beetle larvae cluster on the tender shoots of the tree, as many as 150 on each, and after one day, they begin secreting lac. The males make relatively small lac cells and live a few days outside them, while the females remain confined within their lac cells and live for a number of weeks depending on the weather, locale, etc. During these weeks, the female beetle secretes a large amount of lac until depositing several hundred larvae in her cell. The insect's entire life cycle concludes within four months.

The lac on the tree can be harvested before or after the life cycle of the insect is complete. If harvesting is done before, several sticks covered with lac,

called *broodlac*, can be tied together and used to infect another tree. If the lac is harvested after the insects have died, it is called *sticklac*. Sticklac is then processed into *seedlac*. After being crushed and washed several times, the seedlac can be further refined in one of two ways. High quality lac (*button lac* or shellac flakes) is produced by processes of heating and melting. Lower quality lac, called *garnet lac*, results from dissolving the lac in an alcohol solution and heating this solution until the alcohol evaporates.

Today, a major user of shellac is the hard candy industry. Have you ever noticed how hard candy tends to stick together after it has been sitting out for a while? That's the effect of humidity on the shellac. Shellac tends to soften when humidity is high and will water spot easily.

It's easy to understand why shellac became so popular. It was the major finish of the furniture industry from 1800 to 1925. When French polished, it produces arguably the most beautiful finish available. It resists ultraviolet light better than most oil-based finishes, and if it's tough enough for a bowling alley, it certainly will last on your dining room table. It is easily applied, and by virtue of its solubility in alcohol, damaged shellac finishes can be easily repaired by applying alcohol.

The only secret to using shellac is to mix your own solution using shellac flakes and a fairly pure alcohol solvent. (Denatured alcohol or 190-proof grain alcohol from the liquor store are both appropriate solvents.)

There are some problems inherent to shellac, but these can be readily avoided or easily repaired. Water condensed from vases or drinking glasses can leave white rings on the surface. On younger finishes (less than twenty years old), simply apply denatured alcohol to the affected area, and the water will evaporate as the finish dries. At worst, you may have to apply a light coat of shellac to make the surface uniform. You should also be sure not to place extremely hot objects on your shellacked surface, as the finish will become malleable at about 150 degrees Fahrenheit.

The worst problem that could develop is your shellac finish could dry soft, leaving a tacky, gummy surface. This results from using shellac that has been sitting too long. You can easily avoid this by mixing your own shellac and using it within a fairly short period of time. Finally, the fact that alcohol dissolves shellac means that a spilled martini could dissolve your finish, too.

Shellac Tips

- Shellac dries fast.
- When French finished, or French polished, shellac provides the most beautiful finish available.
- It resists ultraviolet light.
- Shellac is a long-lasting finish.
- It is easily repaired using denatured alcohol.
- Water can leave white rings on a shellac finish.
- Extremely hot objects can damage shellac finishes.
- Shellac can dry soft, leaving a tacky, gummy surface.

Lacquer and Japanning

Lacquer is the most popular finish in furniture today. Actually, it has been the most widely used finish since approximately 1925. It has its roots in Chinese lacquerwork, which has been practiced since at least 1500 B.C. The Chinese made their lacquer from a liquid secreted by the varnish tree, which is related to the common sumac.

When lacquerware first arrived in Europe, Europeans were not able to figure out how it had been produced. They tried several different formulas, featuring varying amounts and types of varnishes and lacs from all over Asia and Europe, but did not discover the true source of lacquer until the end of the seventeenth century. When they tried to import the resin from Asia, it dried too quickly and was useless by the time it arrived in Europe.

The copy of lacquer that the English developed was called *japan*, and used shellac as its base. Japanning became terrifically popular in England, serving as an approved hobby for women in the late 1600s and early 1700s. In fact, japanning was taught as a required class at many of the finishing schools for girls at this time. Japanning produced a dark, sleek surface, which resembled French polish over a painted surface. (French polish, or French finish, used the technique of "padding" on several thin layers of shellac to obtain a high gloss finish.)

Japanned work was a European imitation of Asian lacquer. The European craftsmen couldn't figure out what kind of base the lacquer was made from, so they used the nearest thing they had, which was shellac. The Asian lacquer was based on secretions of the varnish tree, which is native to China. If furniture was to be japanned, stain was not used because the japan gave an opaque finish through which the wood couldn't be seen. Japanned work generally had black as its background color, and red, blue, yellow, and green were commonly used in the foreground.

The japan finish has not stood up well over time. Even the best professionally made pieces have cracked and faded. By the early 1800s, japan had been superseded by shellac and was only used on "fancy chairs." Not until the twentieth century would lacquer be prevalent again.

The home refinisher will not find lacquer as easy to use as the professional does. Lacquer thinner, the solvent for lacquer, contains acetone and dries so quickly that it is difficult to brush lacquer on. Lacquer is best applied by spraying. If you choose to use a spray gun, consult the instructions in Chapter 6.

Polyurethane

Polyurethane is the most popular finish for those who refinish furniture as a hobby. It is very easy to apply and requires little maintenance. You do not have to mix the polyurethane before applying it, and there aren't even any secrets to making it look its best. There are a couple of reasons, however, that you will rarely see a polyurethane finish applied by an experienced professional. Once the finish is on, it cannot be touched up. It can be cleaned and waxed, but if there is a scratch in the finish, the only way to repair it is to refinish the whole piece. Second, while some polyurethane finishes, especially Benjamin Moore One-Hour Finish, dry fairly quickly, polyurethane generally does not dry nearly as quickly as shellac or lacquer.

Isocyanates, intermediate products in the production of polyurethane, were first discovered in 1849. Polyurethane itself was not used much until after World War II. Polyurethane was used to coat airplanes during the war in an effort to find a paint or finish that could stand up to rapidly changing and adverse weather conditions. It proved suitable for this use, but the nylon industry had more to do with the development of polyurethanes as we know them today.

Nylon had been patented by those who first discovered it, and these patents guaranteed them the vast majority of this lucrative market. Scientists who had been hired to find a way to skirt the existing nylon patents ended up stumbling upon many types of polyurethanes, some of which could be used in cloth and fabrics as nylon was, but others of which had properties completely different from those of nylon or any other manmade substance.

One of the reasons for the adaptability of polyurethanes is that the base form of a polyurethane can be easily augmented by attaching additives, which form a chemical bond with the polyurethane. These additives can give almost any property to the polyurethane. Examples relevant to furniture include gloss-modifying additives, ultraviolet-protection additives, and flow-control additives.

Polyurethanes often contain solvents. These are a necessary evil, and producers of polyurethanes try to limit the percentage of solvents as much as possible. These solvents are the reason polyurethane cannot be applied over most other finishes, whether as a finish coat or as a sealer. The solvents present in the polyurethane would eat through the existing finish before the solvents had time to evaporate.

Of all the types of polyurethanes, two specifically are used in the furniture finish industry. These are moisture-cured urethanes and one-component-blocked urethanes. The former are popular because they are ready to use as they come out of the jar. They flow smoothly and give a high gloss finish. They have great flexibility, allowing for the wood beneath to expand and contract, and they are impervious to alcohol. Unfortunately, they do not dry well in some areas, and both sunlight and water can have highly detrimental effects to a finish made of this type of polyurethane.

The one-component-blocked urethanes are unaffected by water and not affected nearly as much by sunlight. Blocked urethanes are also very easy to work with and dry quickly.

Polyurethane Tips

- Polyurethane is the most popular finish for hobbyists.
- It cannot be touched up.
- Most types of polyurethane finishes do not dry quickly.
- Polyurethanes contain solvents.
- They cannot be applied over other finishes.
- There are two types of polyurethanes: moisture-cured and one-component-blocked.

  Moisture-cured polyurethanes flow smoothly, have a high gloss, are flexible, and are impervious to alcohol.

  They do not always dry well.

  Sunlight and water have detrimental effects.

  One-component-blocked polyurethanes are unaffected by water.

  They are not as much affected by sunlight.

  They are easy to work with and quick drying.

Linseed Oil

Linseed oil is produced from the seeds of the flax plant. It can be found in two varieties: raw and boiled. Raw linseed oil never dries and is not suitable for furniture finish. Boiled linseed oil dries slowly, but if you have applied a thin enough coat of oil, it will eventually dry completely. From this point forward, when I refer to linseed oil I specifically mean boiled linseed oil.

Although boiled linseed oil does dry better than raw linseed oil, it is still a good idea to add japan drier (available at most hardware stores) to the oil to speed the drying process. Also, you should dilute the linseed oil with from ¼ to ⅓ mineral spirits, which will have the dual effects of cleaning the surface as you apply the finish and of further speeding the drying process. Turpentine can also be used to dilute the linseed oil, but mineral spirits will dry faster.

Linseed oil takes quite a bit of work to apply and also takes some effort to maintain. Over the course of a couple of days, brush the thinned linseed oil over the workpiece. Try to keep all of the piece wet all of the time. This shouldn't be too difficult, because linseed oil will stay wet for some time. Once the wood has stopped absorbing linseed oil, wipe it down hard with a clean soft cloth. Then allow it to dry in a warm, dry room for approximately ten to fifteen days. Once it has become dry to the touch, you can put it back in place. Then apply the thinned linseed oil with a flannel cloth once a week for six months. Six months is an estimate, but an accurate one. This work builds up the finish. It will not work if the layers you apply are too thick. Then you could be left with a gummy surface. Wipe all the oil you apply off the piece except for an extremely thin layer of finish. Once this six-month period has ended and the finish has developed, the finish may be waxed and cleaned like any other.

Linseed oil provides excellent protection against water and alcohol. In addition, the acids in fruit and vegetable juices will not affect the wood through the linseed oil finish. A final advantage to the linseed oil finish is that it provides an unparalleled deep window to the wood, especially wood that is heavily grained.

There is a warning regarding linseed oil as a finish. It will darken the wood on which it's placed. This occurs for two reasons. First, the oil, like any other liquid, will darken wood. Second, because the oil stays wet for as long as six months, it accrues a lot of dirt. This dirt will obscure the wood below but will also give a look of age to the wood. This darkening is irreversible, however.

One other warning, this time regarding linseed oil as a polish. Never use a polish, cleaner, or wax containing linseed oil. The linseed oil dries by taking in oxygen from the air and actually undergoes a chemical transformation called polymerization. This polymerization bonds the linseed oil so strongly that it will be difficult if not impossible to remove with solvents. If you have a polish you can't remove, you really can't see the finish, let alone clean it. Also, the drying that can be so attractive in a linseed oil finish serves as a blind over the existing finish when it results from a linseed oil polish.

A final note about linseed oil is that it should never be used in conjunction with vinegar or any other acid. The oil will not just darken; it will take on completely different colors due to the presence of the acid. The result can be a chocolatey mess that is too solid to wipe off without damaging the wood beneath, yet not completely solid. The reason I make a point of mentioning that linseed oil polishes should never be used is that Don Williams, furniture curator of the Smithsonian Institution, told me that up until about twenty-five years ago the standard furniture cleaning substance in museums was made of linseed oil, beeswax, turpentine, and vinegar.

Linseed Oil Tips

- Never use raw linseed oil.
- Add japan drier to boiled linseed oil to speed the drying process.
- Dilute linseed oil with ¼ to ⅓ mineral spirits.
- Keep all of the piece wet all the time.
- Allow the piece to dry ten to fifteen days.
- Apply one thinned coat a week for six months.
- Wipe all excess oil off the piece so the finish won't become gummy.
- A linseed oil finish provides excellent protection against water, alcohol, fruit and vegetable juices.
- Linseed oil darkens the wood.
- Never use linseed oil as a polish.
- Don't use linseed oil with vinegar or other acids.

Varnish

Varnish finishes have been around in a variety of forms for over two hundred years. Varnish consists of a resin dissolved in a drying oil (such as linseed or nut oil) or a chemical solvent. Coloring agents can also be added for an opaque finish. Plant materials, indigo, for example, or aniline dyes can be used to color varnish.

Most commercially available varnishes can be used on furniture, but you should not use any product labeled "Spar Varnish" on your furniture. Spar varnish is specifically for outdoor use and will never really dry on your furniture.

Varnish is applied with a bristle brush, and you will need at least two coats for a suitable finish. Varnish tends to dry quite slowly, especially in comparison to shellac and lacquer finishes. You will need to let each coat dry overnight before sanding it with 220 grit sandpaper and applying another coat of varnish.

Because they take so long to dry, varnish finishes tend to accumulate a lot of dust unless care is taken to keep the piece of furniture dust-free. The best way to do this is to work in an uncrowded room with no draft. Another quirk of applying varnish is that it will not dry properly on a cold or damp day. When applying varnish, be careful not to agitate the container or the varnish inside, because if air bubbles form in the varnish, it will not leave a smooth finish.

So far, it sounds as though I have nothing good to say about varnish. While I'll admit it is not my favorite finish, it does provide an attractive and extremely durable finish. Varnish is resistant to water and alcohol, and it is fairly easy to apply, once you have a little experience with it. The main reason that I don't use varnish in my shop is that I can't afford to spray one coat of finish on a piece of furniture and then wait a day before I spray on another coat. Working with lacquer or shellac, I can spray two coats in about fifteen minutes.

If you are a professional, you won't have much use for varnish. It will give a nice look to your furniture if you are an amateur, but a good polyurethane finish would be easier to use and faster to finish.

Varnish Tips

- Apply varnish with a bristle brush.
- You will need to apply at least two coats.
- Varnish dries slowly.
- It will not dry well in a cold or damp environment.
- Don't agitate the varnish container; bubbles will form and leave a finish that is not smooth.
- A varnish finish is resistant to water and alcohol.
- It is fairly easy to apply.

HARMFUL FURNITURE PRODUCTS

Regardless of whether your furniture or cabinets are new or old, there are things that can damage the finish; damage that you can prevent. Preventing the damage from taking place is important, as it will save you time and money in unnecessary repairs and refinishing later. In addition, the finish on your furniture (and therefore your furniture itself) will look much, much better. Here are some of the common problems that can occur and ways to prevent them. (I will discuss repairs to damaged finishes in Chapter 4.)

Harmful furniture products will damage the finish on your furniture. If you ever watch television or walk down an aisle in the supermarket, you have seen many of the products sold and advertised to do wonders for your furniture finish. Out of curiosity, I often read the fine print on the back of many of the cans, which reads "Not for older finishes," and I wonder exactly what this means. Does it mean ten years old, thirty years old, or a hundred years old? Who knows? I don't, but I do know that I see all kinds of products and home remedies being used on furniture that have no business being there.

Every manufacturer is trying to sell you something. You may see a product that is supposed to work quickly, be easy to use, and can be bought off the shelf as you shop for groceries. If I were not in the furniture restoration business, I would most likely be buying the same things and thereby damaging the finish on the furniture in my home.

Over the years, I would deliver pieces I had refinished and would take notice of the furniture in my customers' homes. I often asked, "What do you use to clean and wax your furniture?" The responses I got, and the potentially damaging products lurking in closets and pantries, made me wonder. Why would these good people intentionally use products that would harm the finish on their fine furniture — but that's exactly what was happening.

Problems Resulting from Furniture Waxes and Polishes

There are three types of cleaning products available: aerosol, liquid, and paste wax. My experience has been that the most commonly used of the three are aerosols and liquids. I suppose the reason for this is that they are so easy to use and give a pleasing appearance to the finish, yet they are the most harmful to the finish. Let's take a look at the three types of cleaners or polishes you could use and see how to best maintain the finish on your furniture.

If you consider a piece of your furniture to be of historical value, I recommend you consult an expert before polishing or cleaning it, since the application of wax or polish could cause damage to loose veneer or other unstable surfaces.

AEROSOLS

Using aerosols, the best you can hope for is that they won't damage the finish. Aerosols often contain silicone oils and leave other contaminants behind that will harm the finish. Some "dusting aerosols" may be suitable when applied to a cloth (as opposed to spraying the product directly on the surface of the furniture piece), but the result is no better than using a clean, damp cloth.

LIQUIDS

Liquid polishes can be grouped in two categories. The first, emulsion cleaners/polishes, are water-based products that contain any number of ingredients (waxes, oils, detergents, etc.) suspended in a water solution. This water base makes the product easy to apply and can give the finish a beautiful sheen, but this sheen gradually dissipates as the liquid evaporates.

A second concern is that the contaminants in a liquid solution can have a greater harmful effect than they would in an aerosol, because the contaminants in a liquid solution have more consistent contact with and exposure to the surface.

The second type of liquid polish is oil polish, which is divided into two categories. These are "drying" or "non-drying" oils. Oil polishes can include almost anything among their ingredients, from waxes and oils to perfumes and colorants. The results obtained with oil polishes can be very attractive, but there are problems with both the drying and non-drying oils.

Non-drying oils, as the name suggests, stay damp continually, which means that any dust in the air could end up stuck to your furniture, covering the finish. Other than this characteristic, they are generally harmless. The drying oils, such as linseed and tung oils, bond to the finish of your furniture, making them extremely difficult to remove. In addition, these oil polishes tend to take on a gold or brown hue with age. As dangerous as aerosols can be, they are less troublesome than liquid polishes.

Paste Waxes

Paste wax is by far the best material to use on finished surfaces, especially wood, provided that silicone and other undesirable contaminants are not included in the ingredients. Goddard's, Briwax, Butcher's, and Johnson's paste waxes are all fine products, and there are others. Paste wax does require vigorous buffing, and if you are working on a fragile piece, care must be taken to avoid damaging it by being too forceful. In fact, paste wax may not be appropriate for some very fragile pieces.

If paste wax sounds like a lot of work, remember that a piece may only need to be rewaxed once every three years. A good way to tell when rewaxing is required is if the finish won't buff to a shine with a clean cloth. For example, you may only wax the legs on a table once every three years, but the top may have to be waxed once or twice a year, depending on how heavily it is used.

Testing Products for Harmful Effects

Here is a simple test to give you some idea of the long-term effects of the products you are using on your furniture and its finish. Pour or spray the polish, in quantity, onto a plate. There should be enough polish to form a small pool in the plate. Leave the plate uncovered on a windowsill. Now

simply let the polish stand about two weeks and check to see what happens. What you will want to note is what is left when the liquid evaporates. Does it remain oily for a long period of time? Does it leave a discolored crust in the plate? Well, this is exactly what it will do on your furniture, and who knows what damage it will cause over the long term, depending on the finish.

IMPORTANT! Looking at the products you are using to clean and polish your furniture finish is something you can check today to prevent further damage to the finish. The sooner you do this, the better to protect and preserve the finish. Remember, older pieces that will require refinishing due to deterioration of the original finish will lose value. Also, you will be protecting the other fine pieces of furniture in your home by giving them the care they deserve.

Harmful Furniture Products

- Aerosol cleaners and polishes usually contain silicone oils and other contaminants.
- Liquid polishes are often water based; their sheen will dissipate as the water evaporates.
- Oil polishes may be non-drying or drying. Non-drying oil polishes stay damp and attract dust.

  Drying oils bond to the furniture finish, are very difficult to remove, and darken with age.
- Paste waxes are the best polish material. Look for products *without* silicone.

WHY CLEAN AND WAX YOUR FURNITURE?

I have described the purpose of the finish above, which is to enhance the beauty and protect the wood. Think of wax as doing the same thing for the finish that the finish does for the wood. That is, waxing the finish will enhance its beauty and protect it. Again, a good quality paste wax is the product to use to protect the finish on your wood furniture pieces and to enhance their beauty.

Below, I would like to give some additional tips on areas of your furniture that need to be looked at regularly to check any deterioration of the finish before the finish is irreparably harmed.

Dusting Your Furniture

The best tool for dusting furniture is a feather duster. A feather duster is easier to use than a dust cloth. Most important, the feather duster will remove dust and foreign particles from the surface of the finish, whereas wiping a cloth across the finish can cause minute abrasions to the finish, which, over time, can make the surface of the finish appear dull and lifeless.

Cleaning Your Furniture

If your furniture is only dusty, and doesn't have any other foreign matter on it that needs to be cleaned off, it should simply be dusted with the feather duster as described above. There is no benefit to cleaning dusty furniture with a damp cloth or with furniture cleaner. In fact, doing so may actually be detrimental to the finish. There is no point in putting water in contact with your furniture unless it is absolutely necessary. We have already discussed the potential harmful effects of water-based (as well as oil-based) cleaning products.

The purpose of cleaning is to remove foreign material, such as fingerprints, food particles, etc., from the finish. Cleaning should be done with a damp cloth or a cloth sprayed lightly with Endust. Don't soak the cloth with water. By a damp cloth, I mean a cloth not so wet that it would need to be wrung out.

A word of advice: Dust to your heart's content, but clean only when it is needed. Extra dusting won't hurt the finish, but extra cleaning can.

Waxing Your Furniture

Waxing, as stated above, protects the finish and enhances its beauty. It may help you remember this if you think not of waxing your *furniture* but only of waxing the *finish*.

Older, fragile finishes require more care than the newer high-tech finishes. Because of hardness and resistance to water and alcohol, new furniture finishes do not require as much care to preserve their beauty.

Waxing becomes necessary when rubbing with a soft cloth does not produce a sheen on the furniture piece. The best wax to use on your furniture is paste wax, and there are many good name-brand paste waxes available at most hardware stores. Paste waxing is more time consuming than wiping your furniture down with oil that smells like a lemon, but the beauty of paste-waxed wood cannot be matched by aerosol or liquid waxes.

And while paste waxing your furniture takes longer, it will only be necessary, in many cases, once every three years. Top surfaces that need to be cleaned often (as opposed to simply dusting them) may need to be waxed more frequently.

Paste wax should be applied with a clean, soft cloth. Care should be taken to apply small amounts at a time. A lighter application of paste wax will be easier to buff to a shine than a heavy application, which can become a mess. Apply the paste wax with one cloth and buff with another clean, soft cloth. Lint-free cloths are best to use when working with paste wax. An old T-shirt is excellent.

Cleaning and Waxing Tips

- Dust with a feather duster — it won't abrade the furniture surface.
- Clean with a damp (not wet) cloth or a cloth sprayed lightly with Endust.
- It is time to wax when rubbing with a soft cloth does not produce a sheen.
- Paste wax only as needed with a clean, soft cloth, applying small amounts of wax at a time.

SOURCES OF DAMAGE TO YOUR FURNITURE

What's in a Fingerprint?

What's in a fingerprint that will damage the finish on your furniture? That's the question I had for a Charlottesville, Virginia, dermatologist. He told me that in addition to dirt, hand cream, perfume, and anything else your fingers touch, fingerprints have sweat as a main ingredient. Sweat includes chloride, sodium, potassium, and urea (all of which are salts). Lactic acid is another major ingredient of sweat.

Areas of the finish that are touched frequently accumulate a build-up of all these, which creates a chemical reaction that begins to break down the finish underneath. The longer fingerprints stay on the finish, the more time the finish has to break down. It begins to turn dark as the moist salts attract dirt. At this point, severe damage is being done to the finish underneath.

The next time you feel a soft, sticky finish on a chair arm and can scrape it off with your fingernail, you will know what has caused that damage and why. To detect this problem, look for a change in the sheen from the other surrounding finish or just make a point of regularly cleaning areas frequently touched by fingerprints.

Water

Excessive use of water can damage a finish, especially if it's an older shellac or lacquer finish. Earlier I recommended that you use a damp cloth to clean your furniture, and now I want to emphasize that "damp" does not mean "wet." You should clean your furniture with a soft cloth *moistened* with water, but not to the point that it is necessary to wring it out. Most of us have seen the damage a water glass left on a table can cause.

It should be noted that cleaning your furniture with water or products that you mix with water can cause serious problems to the finish and the wood underneath. White rings and milky finishes caused by water are due to the finish absorbing the water and creating a cloud.

Several products currently on the market advertised as wood cleaners direct you to mix them with water before use. These may work for a very few finishes, but for most they are a potential disaster. The only exception is if you know exactly what the finish is and that cleaning it with a watery solution will not harm it. Many concentrated products that are promoted for cleaning the wood finishes in your home may be fine for the floors, but they can be very harmful to any furniture finish.

Sunlight

Sunlight, especially ultraviolet radiation, can do serious damage to the finish on your furniture. Sunlight can penetrate through a clear finish like shellac and bleach the wood underneath. An opaque finish affected by sunlight can end up looking washed out. Light in general can be harmful to furniture. Fluorescent bulbs give off more ultraviolet light than incandescent bulbs, so the latter are certainly preferable for your furniture. Bulbs of both types are available shaded so as to limit the amount of ultraviolet light they release.

Sources of Damage

- Fingerprints, over time, will create a chemical reaction with the finish that turns it dark and then attracts dirt.
- Use a damp, not wet, cloth to clean furniture.
- Do not use furniture cleaning/waxing products containing water.
- Avoid direct sunlight on furniture.

MYTHS ABOUT WOOD

Earlier I talked about the products to "clean and wax" your furniture. All the claims made on labels would lead you to believe that these products are great for the care of your furniture. In fact, the reverse is true. When I see commercials on television advertising furniture products, I have to shake my head in disgust at the claims made. I suppose the ads and labels are bad enough, but still there are myths floating around that many people truly believe about their furniture and wood.

Myth #1: Wood Is Alive

The wood in your furniture is not alive. When the wood was in the forest and still part of a living tree, the vast majority of the wood cells were dead. After being cut, the few remaining live cells die. By the time the wood is delivered to a cabinet or furniture maker, it has been dried and dead for a long time.

Myth #2: Wood Needs to Breathe

The wood in your furniture or cabinets does not breathe. There is no need to have air circulate at the surface of the wood, and applying wax or a finish will not harm the wood.

Myth #3: Wood and Finishes Need to Be Fed

It is not necessary or recommended to "feed" or "nourish" wood or wood finishes. The wood is not alive and, therefore, cannot be fed. If your furniture looks dry and lifeless, a new finish can be applied or the existing finish can be cleaned and waxed.

Myth #4: As Wood Ages, Moisture and Natural Oils Must Be Replaced

First, most woods do not have oils. If the wood does contain natural oils, they in no way affect the preservation of the piece, and they cannot be matched by oils commercially available. Claims that oil can replace water in the wood are completely untrue. Oil and water cannot mix and cannot replace each other.

Second, the moisture in the wood will not be lost if the piece is at equilibrium moisture content with its surrounding environment. In fact, adding water could cause serious damage to the wood as the rapid change in moisture content can make the wood split.

Who knows where these myths started? One place I think they might have come from is the minds of people trying to sell you products to do "miracles" for the finish. Whether in the 1890s or the 1990s, claims made for products are not always to be believed. All you have to do is turn on the TV or walk down the aisle in the supermarket, and you will see firsthand how myths have been promulgated. Look for products claiming to "feed" either the finish or the wood. In most cases, I believe you could do just as well by mixing a can of 30 or 40 weight (your preference) motor oil and kerosene to achieve the same effect. It's possible that this mixture could be less damaging to the finish than many of the products in your local supermarket, and it would cost less, too. Don't quote me on the motor oil. I don't want to start yet another myth about using motor oil and kerosene on furniture.

THE BEST CONDITIONS FOR YOUR FURNITURE

The best possible condition for your furniture would be in a dark room with a clean sheet over it. The temperature would be 70 degrees Fahrenheit, and the relative humidity would be 50%. The room would be free of insects and mammals of all types, including people. This means the furniture would never be touched by human hands nor see the light of day.

We all know the above is not an option, unless you plan to keep your furniture in the Great Pyramid and never see it. Since you want to use your furniture, here is a practical guide to help you compensate for the inevitable deterioration of your furniture.

Insects, humidity, and sunlight all can damage your furniture, but most damage to furniture is done by people. Of that damage, most is done by using improper products to clean and wax the finish.

CARING FOR HISTORICAL FURNITURE

Caring for your furniture takes on added significance for pieces with historical value. Collectible furniture has both aesthetic value and investment value, but its financial value can be endangered or limited by how it is cared for. The financial value of a piece of furniture is determined by several factors; chief among them are rarity, condition, maker, and historical relevance. The condition and historical relevance of a piece are the only elements of its value that a collector can affect. Don Williams, head Furniture Conservator at the Smithsonian Institution, recommends *conservation* of the furniture as the best method of maximizing its value.

Conservation

Conservation tries to balance the factors of historical and aesthetic value, as exemplified in the "six foot-six inch rule." This rule holds that repairs to collectible pieces should not be noticeable from a distance of six feet, but that a trained eye could spot evidence of repairs from only six inches away. Some of the elements of conservation hold true for pieces not considered "collectible" but still valued by their owners. For example, the materials used on your furniture should be as stable as possible. If you could polish your furniture once every three years as opposed to once a month, and take better care of

it by doing so, why wouldn't you? In the long run, poor repairs or care will cost you far more than repairs done well.

SUMMARY: CARING FOR THE FINISH ON YOUR FURNITURE

- Know the products that you are using on your furniture to ensure they will not harm the finish.
- Dust your furniture with a feather duster.
- To clean your furniture, use a damp cloth or a cloth sprayed with Endust.
- Check areas that are touched frequently, such as chair arms, chair backs, table tops, bedposts, and the area around cabinet pulls, among others. Make sure these areas are kept clean to prevent deterioration of the finish.
- Use a good paste wax when you determine waxing is necessary.

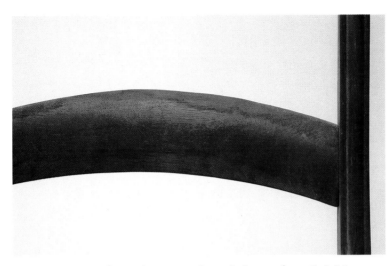

This chair back looks as though it needs refinishing.

Cleaning the chair back with hand cleaner and fine steel wool.

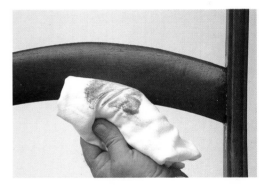

Buffing with a cloth will remove the dirt lifted by the hand cleaner and give the finish a new sheen.

This table base looks dull and lifeless.

Waxing the finish with Briwax and fine steel wool.

The final buffing brings out the beauty of the piece.

This cabinet door shows water damage typical of doors in the sink area.

Minwax stain is brushed on with a sponge brush.

Excess stain is wiped off with a cloth.

Tiny specks, here a spot of paint, can be gently removed with a pocket knife.

Touching up the chips with the sponge brush.

The result — in less than five minutes.

This chair belonged to President James Monroe. The veneer on its front edge is chipped in two places. If you are not ready to undertake a difficult veneer repair, a simple touchup can make a big difference.

Denatured alcohol is applied with a rag in several quick passes.

A closeup of the same Monroe chair. The lighter areas indicate water damage.

The alcohol has revived the shellac finish.

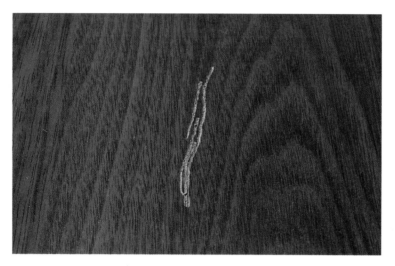

The scratch on this table top will be repaired using the burn-in technique. Don't try this without the help of a professional.

Using 400-grit sandpaper on a block to level the finish.

Shellac sticks come in different colors.

The heated shellac stick is melted into the scratch.

Heating the shellac stick.

Leveling the burn-in balm.

Applying burn-in balm protects the shellac stick from sticking to other areas of the finish.

Sanding again to level.

French padding the finish.

The final finish. Where is the scratch?

This small rocker has a badly chipped edge.

Using Bartley Gel Finish on a sponge brush to touch up the chipped edge.

This process took about two minutes.

The arm of this rocking chair is badly damaged by body oil.

Sanding will help the stain penetrate rather than lying on the surface.

The stain should be brushed lightly to achieve an even, dark color.

The drawer guide. Note the drawer glide is missing.

This chest is a good candidate for refinishing, but note the drawers are tilted back. The drawer glide needs work.

The replacement drawer glide in place.

This rocking chair has a broken arm.

The center of the spindle has been drilled out and filled out with epoxy to accept the new screw. It will be stronger than before when dry.

The chair arm repaired.

Applying paint remover with the
grain, from end to end of the piece.

Brushing into the finish, it
becomes obvious that the
paint remover has
reacted and the finish is
loosening.

Wiping off the old finish
and paint remover.

The final wipe-down
ensures all the old finish
is removed.

A lac beetle — the source of shellac.

2.
Protect the Investment in Your Furniture

Maintaining the investment you have in your furniture will not be as hard as you might think. As an incentive to maintain your furniture, think how much you would have to spend if you had to go out today and replace every single piece of furniture in your home.

When I think of protecting the investment of furniture in your home, three things come to mind. First, is your furniture properly insured? Do you have documentation and photographs of your furniture? Is this documentation in a safe, fireproof place so that in the event of a fire or theft it can be retrieved? A video camera would be an excellent way to document your furnishings, along with bills of sale or estimates of value.

Second, is the history of the piece documented? The history of the piece may include such items as who made the piece, when it was made, who the previous owners were, etc. Just as important as the answers to these questions is the story behind the piece of furniture. The story and significance of the piece may be lost forever if anything should happen to its owner, unless this information is documented as carefully as any important financial information. Will your heirs know what significance certain special pieces have if you aren't there to tell them?

Compiling this documentation will bring back many good memories of family and friends that will keep their memories alive for you and your heirs. It will add to and protect that special meaning of those pieces that you pass on.

The third way to protect the investment in your furniture is to maintain the condition and structure of your furniture in order to slow down its deterioration as much as possible. Remember, all things deteriorate, and the best we can do is to slow the process. If you wish to slow the process of the deterioration of your furniture, you can do so with some knowledge. You need to:

- Use the appropriate products to care for the finish on your furniture;
- Know where to look for problem areas that may suddenly arise;
- Find ways to make your furniture function better and be easier to use; and
- Prevent small problems from becoming major ones.

INSURANCE

Make sure your furniture investment is adequately covered by the homeowner's insurance policy in effect on your home. (If you rent and do not have renter's insurance, look into it right away.) Check with your insurance agent to determine whether your coverage is sufficient for any pieces of exceptional value. Should those pieces be covered in a separate rider to your existing policy?

DOCUMENTING YOUR FURNITURE

There are more than financial considerations to take into account when evaluating your furniture. Documentation of your furniture serves many purposes. It can protect the monetary value of the furniture for you and your heirs, and it maintains the story behind each piece of furniture. The history of a piece enhances its value, whether to the family who owns it or to a collector.

Most furniture has value. Some pieces may be of such great value that no price could be put on their worth. Others have potential for looking great in your home, but they may require refinishing. Often these are the pieces people have in their basements or garages; the pieces belonged to their grandparents and haven't been used for some time. These are often the most fun pieces I get to work on. Others will be of less value or no value, pieces discarded or hauled to the dump and deemed worthless because the time and money to repair missing or broken parts may far outweigh their value.

For insurance purposes, for your heirs, and for your own peace of mind, you should have complete documentation of any valuable pieces of furniture in your home. That value need not necessarily be monetary; it could be simply the sentimental value you place on a particular piece for its heritage or associations. Many pieces of furniture in your home have special personal meaning and value to you, which could be lost without documentation and recordkeeping.

I have oak thumb back chairs in my breakfast room that belonged to my Grandmother and Grandfather Haney. How well I remember these chairs being in my grandparents' home, and how they bring back all the special moments I spent with them. These chairs aren't of any particular monetary value, but

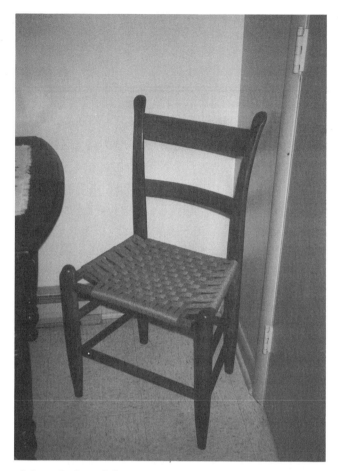

My oak thumb back chairs may have little value to someone else, but are priceless to me because of their associations.

they have great value to me as they belonged to my grandparents and were given to me by them. It would be sad for me to think that if something were to happen to me today or tomorrow, the story behind these chairs would be lost forever.

Records

Maintain written records of your furniture pieces. These records should include the following:

- date purchased or received
- where purchased
- purchase price paid
- provenance; i.e., previous owner(s)
- appraisals
- conservation or restoration techniques
- complete description

*This bed was used in the White House but has no documentation to support this;
its value is consequently reduced.*

This desk I restored was a gift from James Madison to James Monroe. Its value is based on the documentation of this fact.

The description of the piece should include when it was made, by whom it was made, the types of materials included, any signs of damage or previous restoration, the style of the piece, its dimensions, and any other pertinent information. A sample documentation form and a blank documentation form are included for your use on pages 38 and 39.

Art Restoration Services offers a complete kit to get you started in documenting your possessions. Their address is:

Art Restoration Services
P.O. Box 2608
Charlottesville VA 22902
(800) 484-7746

Photograph or Video Documentation

There are two ways to approach a visual documentation of a piece of furniture. The first is to take photographs of it. It is helpful to photograph the piece from several angles. If the piece is of an unusual size, you may want to show a yardstick in the photo as a point of reference.

Try to take the photographs against a neutral background if at all possible. (Obviously, you are not going to move a dining room table that seats twenty just to get a neutral background.) If the furniture piece has any unusual detail — elaborate carving, a secret drawer — take close-up photos of that too.

The other method, which is becoming increasingly popular, is to make a video documentation of your furniture. The simplest way to do this is to walk around your home, shooting the video of the particular pieces of furniture as you go. Before you begin, you should prepare the written documentation of each piece and have it ready to read out loud as you shoot the video.

You don't have to be an expert with a video camera to do this. Just remember to shoot from all angles and move close in as necessary. Video is a great way to give a more personal touch to your documentation. You will sound very natural, as you retell stories about each piece of furniture.

If you decide to create video documentation of your furniture, be sure to have the written documentation

as well. You will also want to have at least one extra copy of the video made for safekeeping.

Where to Keep Your Documentation

There is no point in going to the trouble of creating the documentation of your furniture if you do not keep it in a safe place. You may want to keep one copy — videos or photos and written records — in your home. If so, buy a container that is at minimum fireproof and preferably waterproof as well. You should also keep one copy of your documentation in your safety deposit box or, at the very least, at the home of a trusted friend.

A GUIDE TO EVALUATING YOUR FURNITURE

Historical Value

Who could put a value on a table where President George Washington ate or the rocking chair that sat in the Oval Office when John F. Kennedy was president? These pieces are of great value because of the people who used them. There are many pieces whose historical value is based on where they were or who used them, now or in the past. What wood they are made of and the craftsmanship involved to make them are of little importance; it's the person and/or the place in history that give the pieces their value.

Antique

Age alone is the determining factor as to whether a piece is an antique or not. Antique furniture has attained an age of one hundred years or more. Like other furniture, value is affected by how rare the piece may be and its quality.

Family Heirloom

How can you replace your grandfather's Morris chair or your great grandmother's secretary? Once these pieces are gone from the family, they may be never retrieved again and lost to your family forever. A chair that may have little monetary value may be of great value to you or your family simply because of the family member who owned it. As mentioned before, the simple thumb back chairs in

DOCUMENTATION FORM

—— Sample ——

Furniture Piece _Armoire_

Date Purchased/Received _inherited November 1992_

Place Purchased _—_

Purchase Price Paid _—_

Description of Piece _early 20th century mahogany armoire. Carved top, mirror on each door, Brass hardware. No maker's name._

Provenance (list previous owners' names, addresses, etc., if known)

P. Weiss, 39 University Way

N. W. Binns, 1407 Virginia Avenue

Ann Cloud, address unknown, but probably a family piece of hers originally

Appraisal Information _____

Done by _____

Date appraised _____

Appraised value _____

Restoration/Conservation Techniques (describe in detail, including date procedures done)

delivered to Brad Hughes, Charlottesville, for restoration May 27, 1993

Historical Information _unknown_

Photo or Video Available _photo in safe deposit box_

DOCUMENTATION FORM

Furniture Piece _____

Date Purchased/Received _____

Place Purchased _____

Purchase Price Paid _____

Description of Piece _____

_____

_____

_____

_____

Provenance (list previous owners' names, addresses, etc., if known)

_____

_____

_____

_____

_____

Appraisal Information _____

Done by _____

Date appraised _____

Appraised value _____

Restoration/Conservation Techniques (describe in detail, including date procedures done)

_____

_____

_____

_____

Historical Information _____

_____

_____

_____

_____

Photo or Video Available _____

my breakfast room belonged to my grandparents, and I remember them in their home. They would be of little value to others but bring back many special memories to me of two wonderful people in my life.

Fine Workmanship

Many pieces constructed of fine woods with quality workmanship will have value. Regardless of age, these pieces appreciate in value. I have often heard people say, "You can't get the quality in furniture that you could years ago." This is simply not true. Quality pieces of furniture are available today just as they were in 1790 or 1890. Top quality furniture is much more expensive today than lower quality work just as it was two hundred years ago.

Fine Quality Wood

Beautiful pieces may be constructed of fine quality and/or exotic wood that may be constructed in the most basic ways. A coffee table may have a wooden top constructed of fine finished rosewood or mahogany with a metal base supporting it.

Unique Furniture

My Victrola would not qualify for any of the above categories, yet I enjoy and value it as an interesting piece that is fun to own. An interesting conservation piece is often valued simply for the enjoyment it brings into your home. I often play an old 78 record on the Victrola when friends come over to visit.

Lots of Potential

Many pieces can be improved by a change of stain color or by some creative painting done on the piece. A lot of pieces made in the 1950s are constructed of maple or cherry with a very orange stain color. When the orange stain is changed to a shade more in the brown tones, the piece will be greatly improved in value and appearance. A creative, artistic eye can often bring new life and beauty to pieces of moderate or little value.

Functional Furniture

The piece may simply serve as one with a function that makes it enjoyable to own — the chair you like because it's comfortable to sit in as you do your

work, or the desk with just the right spots for your letters and stationery. The piece may not be a centerpiece in your living room but serves you well in its place.

Waiting to Be Replaced

A woman told me she did not like her table and had no interest in spending any money to improve or restore its looks. She wanted a new table. What else needs to be said? If she sells her old table to get rid of it, it may become a piece with lots of potential to its new owner. Other pieces may be deemed worthless because the cost of the repairs needed would far exceed the value of the piece.

Each piece of furniture in your home will fall into at least one of the above categories. The desk in your study may have been owned by your grandfather and constructed of fine wood and with fine workmanship. It may not matter what an antique dealer offers you for it as a fine antique: it belonged to your granddad, it can't be replaced, and you have no thought of selling it.

The furniture you own is valued by you; you own it and you can do with it as you please. I know of no law that will prevent you from burning every piece of furniture you own in the fireplace if you so desire. But let's hope you're not interested in your furniture as fuel on a cold night. You value your furniture and want it to retain or improve in value. Whether for maintenance, restoration, refinishing, or repair, the money you invest in your furniture should be well spent.

PREVENTIVE MAINTENANCE GUIDE FOR YOUR FURNITURE

Cleaning and Waxing

Most furniture cleaning can be done with a damp cloth, but when heavier cleaning is required, such as in your kitchen, you will need a product such as DL Blue Label Hand Cleaner or Endust. Keeping the finish clean will prevent its deterioration.

Most furniture pieces don't even need to be waxed. They would be better off left alone, as long as they are cleaned periodically. A good example is seeing someone buy new quality furniture and immediately rub oils and waxes on it. This will simply cause deterioration of the finish. Paste waxing these pieces wouldn't hurt, but it would be completely unnecessary. Waxing should be done on a periodic basis, depending on use, with a high quality paste wax.

Checking Potential Problem Areas

Potential problem areas are of two types. The first are areas that hands touch often; the second are those areas exposed to sunlight. Areas that are touched often — chair backs, chair arms, bedposts, etc. — should be inspected on a periodic basis (perhaps two or three times per year) to prevent a build-up of body oil.

There is only one way to prevent sunlight damage, and that is not to expose the piece to sunlight at all. You may wish to avoid having some of your favorite or more valuable pieces exposed to direct sunlight or to have blinds or shades drawn during the day to prevent sunlight damage.

Preventing Drawer Wear

One of the most common types of damage that is done to a chest of drawers as it ages is that the drawer glides wear out. As the drawers are pulled in and out, the glides rub against each other and wear down. If you have ever noticed sawdust in your chest of drawers, this may be from the drawer glides wearing. Removing the drawer and applying paste wax to the drawer glide will help slow this wear and make the drawer much easier to move in and out.

Repairing Early, Before It's Broken

Repairs done early can be done at much lower cost than when the piece is beyond repair. This is not always possible, but if your chairs are loose, they will be much easier to repair when they are simply loose than when they have finally broken.

Although doing repairs early will be easier and less expensive, repairs that you may do improperly will be even more difficult to correct by a craftsman. Take care not to devalue your furniture by doing improper repairs or using incorrect refinishing techniques.

Choosing a Craftsman

When choosing a craftsman to work on your furniture, pick someone you trust who has knowledge and experience. Often for the same money a less talented person would charge, you can have the best do a high quality job.

A craftsman who does not know how to revive an old finish will not suggest this option to you. Many, many pieces are stripped for no reason other than the owner and craftsman are not aware that they can easily be restored.

One of the best learning experiences I've had in recent years was a trip to the Smithsonian Institute to meet with Don Williams, Senior Furniture Conservator. Don took time from his busy schedule to give me and my research assistant, Patrick O'Rourke, a tour through the furniture lab. He did his best to answer a list of questions we had prepared and provided us with hundreds of pages of literature he had written or accumulated on furniture and furniture finishes. Patrick and I left the Smithsonian feeling we had met a public servant, one with a heartfelt desire to pass on his vast knowledge of furniture to those interested.

The trip to the Smithsonian and discussions with Don Williams greatly enhanced my respect for furniture. I gained an appreciation for not just antique or historical pieces, but for the quality, craftsmanship, and value that are inherent to many pieces I have the opportunity to work on or see in homes in my community.

Ten years ago I had refinished a table and chairs for customers who had moved to Charlottesville to retire. They asked me to look at a desk they had in their basement den. The desk was a piece that had been in their family for years and they were interested to know if I could tell them whether the desk had any value.

It took only minutes to determine that the desk was a 1770 Chippendale worth at least ten thousand dollars. It was in remarkably good condition but would not stay that way long, sitting in the basement exposed to high humidity. At first sight, one would think the old desk needed lots of work and refinishing to be presentable enough to use in their living room. They wanted to use the desk but did not feel that they would want to invest the money it would take to restore it. What they didn't know was how simple and inexpensive the project would be. A gentle cleaning of the old finish, touching up a few nicks and scratches, and finally a coat of paste wax and the desk was in beautiful condition and removed from the basement and taken upstairs to the living room.

The process to restore the desk took about an hour and cost less than $15. One can of DL Blue Label Hand Cleaner ($1.95), one package of superfine steel wool ($2.50), and a container of Goddard's paste wax ($7.50) were all the supplies required. The finish was cleaned with the Hand Cleaner and superfine steel wool, then buffed with a clean, dry cloth. (Often this is all that will be required.) A light coat of paste wax was applied to add beauty, luster, and protection. In this case, the piece was worth thousands, but regardless, the restoration only cost pennies compared to what an unnecessary refinishing job would have cost. You probably have furniture in your home whose looks can be greatly improved for pennies.

Learning about the furniture in your home, especially the older pieces, is interesting and may en-hance its value to you, regardless of whether the pieces need work or are in excellent condition.

SUMMARY: PROTECTING THE INVESTMENT IN YOUR FURNITURE

- Document for insurance purposes, for your heirs, in case of theft, fire, or other disaster.
- Keep written records as well as photo and/or video documentation.
- Keep all documentation records in a safety deposit box or other very safe place.
- Keep your furniture's finish clean to prevent deterioration.
- Wax only when it is needed.
- Check areas touched frequently to prevent build-up of body oil.
- Check your furniture for damage from sunlight.
- Prevent drawer glide wear by waxing the glides every couple of years.
- Repair early, before a small problem becomes a big one.
- Choose a furniture repair person or refinisher/restorer as carefully as you choose your furniture.

Part II

Restoring and Refinishing Furniture and Cabinets

3.
Reviving Old Finishes

Does your furniture need a tune-up or an overhaul? My wife stopped at a service station to fill her car with gas and asked the attendant about a tapping noise coming from under the hood. The mechanic on duty listened to the noise and told her the cam shaft was going bad and that she should park the car until it was fixed. He told also her that replacing the cam would cost $1,500. That afternoon she told me of her stop at the gas station but that she had decided to take the car to the dealer for his evaluation.

The dealer had a mechanic evaluate the tap, and as a result she was told that the valves needed a simple adjustment at a cost of less than $100. The valves were adjusted, the car runs and sounds great, and we saved $1,400.

What does a car tune-up have to do with the furniture in your home? You have figured this one out already, but I'll state it anyway. A tune-up just may restore the finish on your furniture with better results than a complete overhaul would.

Unfortunately, there are few remaining pieces of historical furniture that have escaped refinishing. What is sad here is that many pieces are refinished simply because the owner or the craftsman doing the refinishing has no experience with reviving old finishes. My question is this: How can the old be given new life if you or the craftsman you engage are not familiar with either the idea that the original finish can be restored or the processes to do so?

WHY TRY REVIVING AN OLD FINISH?

In the color section of this book, there are photos of a chair belonging to President James Monroe's granddaughter. Look at the finish on the chairback pictured. The chair was acquired by Ash Lawn-Highland because it was in the Monroe family. The finish has a streaked, milky look. Someone cleaned the chair using too much water; the result is that the heavy application of water has clouded the finish.

Many years ago, I believed the only solution to repairing this finish would be to refinish it. But I have since learned otherwise. Leave the paint remover at the hardware store! The finish can be restored without stripping the chair and in much less time than it would take to refinish it. Unnecessary refinishing cannot be prevented if you take your furniture to a person who does not know how to restore an old finish.

There are processes that can be used to give new life to many old finishes. The process chosen to revive a finish depends on what type of finish it is and what has caused it to deteriorate. Reviving a finish may require one or more of the processes listed below.

A finish may have deteriorated to such a degree that it cannot be revived. However, a finish that looks as if it has deteriorated to the point that it needs to be stripped may often be revived using the correct techniques and materials.

Reviving old finish is one of the easiest things I have learned to do. I suppose the hardest thing to learn may be which finishes can be revived and which simply need to be stripped off. If you try reviving the old finish first, it won't cost much or take much time, and you will learn which finishes can be revived and which cannot.

FURNITURE WITH HISTORICAL VALUE

Working on the furniture that you use daily is different from working on pieces you think may have historical value. I have done a great deal of work on furniture at Ash Lawn-Highland, President James Monroe's home just outside of Charlottesville, Virginia. While these pieces require repairs similar to those I do all the time at my shop, I go about them more cautiously at Ash Lawn. While any Federal-style chair has value as an antique, a Federal-style chair that was used at the White House has greater value, because it is an object of historic interest. Its value extends beyond simply the value of a beautiful two-hundred-year-old chair; it gains value from its association with a former president. If you have a piece of furniture you think may have historical value, act conservatively and consult a professional furniture restorer before taking action.

When dealing with a piece of historical furniture, there are steps that can be taken to try to maximize its aesthetic value at no cost to its historical value. The first and simplest approach is to do nothing beyond stabilizing the piece's physical environment. Maintaining consistent temperature and humidity decreases stress on the finish.

The least extreme action you can take to change the object's appearance is cleaning it. If the finish is so fragile that rubbing with a cloth would be likely to do more harm than good, several mild detergents are available, which can be dissolved in petroleum thinner or denatured alcohol and applied gently with cotton swabs. A final cleaning option is the use of a gel cleaner, which would fill all the cracks and crevices of the surface without saturating it. Once

the gel has formed a relatively stiff shell on the surface, you can simply peel it off.

If the damage is so serious or the finish so deteriorated that even a gel cleaner will not work without doing more harm than good, I recommend that you consult a conservator or professional refinisher before proceeding.

GUIDE TO REVIVING FINISHES

In reviving old or deteriorated finishes, the steps that may be taken are as follows:

1. Cleaning the finish.
2. Cleaning and waxing the finish.
3. Using solvents to revive the finish.
4. Using stain to revive the finish.
5. Applying new finish over the old finish.

Cleaning the Finish

Last fall I held a seminar at a local library to talk about furniture care and restoration. I had planned to talk about furniture care, touchups, reviving old finishes, repairs, and the refinishing process. The seminar was to last from 7:00 in the evening until 8:30. I thought this would be plenty of time to briefly discuss and take questions on each of these topics. It wasn't.

I wanted to demonstrate how a finish that looked in dire need of refinishing could be restored, and how simple the process was to restore it. The project was an old walnut chair that a friend had given me several years ago. It was on a deck in my shop along with numerous other pieces that I intended to work on at some point. Besides problems with the finish, it was in need of numerous repairs. (I will discuss those in the chapter on repairs.)

I'll never forget how terrible that chair looked when we walked down the aisle with it, showing it to the people so they could see firsthand how bad its condition was. It was just the type of find I loved to discover at a yard sale or used furniture store, a piece that could be purchased and restored for a few dollars. So my assistant walked up and down the aisle showing the folks this chair that most thought would need hours of repair and a complete refinishing job.

Here's where the fun began. Having seen the chair close up, I told everyone that we would repair the chair without using tools and restore the finish while they watched. Now, friends, this is not magic, but if you had been there to see the results you might have thought so.

Remember, the finish is a window to the wood. If the window can't be seen through clearly, the look of the wood will be distorted. I have been restoring furniture for more than twenty years, and it took me several years to begin to understand how many finishes could be restored without stripping them off. If I had come across that chair I had at the seminar in my early years in business, I would have stripped it, sanded it, and gone through all the other involved steps of refinishing to get it to look better. But not this chair. It was saved from the stripper and the sanding. Thank goodness!

The first thing we did to revive the old finish was to get it clean. Now you may think that cleaning a very dirty old finish involves mixing up a gallon of warm water or buying a gallon of turpentine — it doesn't. The way we cleaned this chair could have been done in your living room with a newspaper on the floor. (If I were doing it, I wouldn't even bother with the newspaper.) We used superfine steel wool (you may choose to use a piece of an old towel instead of steel wool) and hand cleaner. The type we used was DL Blue Label Hand Cleaner (which has a mineral spirit base), but others may work as well as long as they do not contain grit. (This will not be the last time you hear about hand cleaner.) With this and several clean rags for buffing, it took about fifteen minutes to do a first-rate cleaning job on our chair. Now with just this cleaning of the finish, the results were great and were a great surprise to the people attending the seminar.

Remember, all we had used was hand cleaner and superfine steel wool. The cost of reviving the finish on this chair was pennies. This is an example of the type of project that often gets stripped unnecessarily. Using one can of DL Blue Label Hand Cleaner and one package of superfine steel wool, I could restore the finish on twenty chairs in similar condition. The steel wool and DL Blue Label Hand Cleaner cost $4.00, so that's about 50 cents per chair!

If you paid someone to *refinish* the chair, it would cost about $75.00. If you bought the supplies and did it yourself, you should plan to spend about $20.00 and several hours of your time. The most important thing to remember is this: this chair didn't need to be refinished. It didn't need to be refinished because the finish was hidden by dirt and grime that came off when it was clean. It was only then that I could determine what further steps, if any, would be needed to restore the finish on this old chair. We decided that the finish would look a little better if it were waxed, so that's all we did.

The big bonus is this. The chair looks better than if it had been completely refinished in my shop. With all the tools, products, and know-how that I have at my disposal, I would be hard pressed to make the chair finish look as good as it did at the seminar, with just cleaning and waxing.

Remember to think of the finish on the wood as a window that you are looking through to the wood. Different environmental factors, human contact, and previous treatments can affect the window so you cannot see through it. If you can't see through the window to the wood clearly because it is in some way distorted or blurred, the piece of furniture will appear to need refinishing.

Reviving an Old Finish With Hand Cleaner

Here is a list of the items you will need to clean a dirty finish that appears to need refinishing:

Supplies

One piece of superfine (00000) steel wool

One can DL Blue Label Hand Cleaner (others may work, but DL Blue Label Hand Cleaner can be finished over later, if necessary)

Clean cloth

The Process

Apply hand cleaner to the steel wool and rub the piece gently to remove any dirt or grime. Then buff with the clean cloth.

CLEANING AND WAXING THE FINISH

Supplies

One piece of super fine (00000) steel wool

Furniture paste wax, such as Goddard's or Briwax (the latter comes in a variety of colors, which can further enhance your furniture's beauty)

Clean cloth

The Process

Apply the wax to the finish with the steel wool, using moderate pressure. Then buff with the clean cloth. Special note: Finishes can be revived with wax, but if applying new finish is required, the wax will prevent the new finish from bonding with the original. Mineral spirits will effectively remove the wax. Only then may new finish be applied.

Using Solvents to Revive the Finish

The two finishes that can be revived using solvents are shellac and lacquer. Shellac can be revived using denatured alcohol, and while lacquer can be revived using solvents, the solvents must be sprayed or padded onto the lacquer finish.

REVIVING A SHELLAC FINISH

Supplies

Denatured alcohol

Clean cloth

The most common finish used prior to 1925 was shellac. Shellac will amalgamate when it comes in contact with denatured alcohol, which means it dissolves and re-forms. Thus, shellac can be revived by putting a small amount of denatured alcohol on a clean cloth and quickly rubbing the cloth across the finish. Only one or two passes should be made across the finish to amalgamate it. It should then be allowed to re-harden for a few minutes. Keep in mind that denatured alcohol, used to excess, will completely remove a shellac finish.

Before you begin amalgamating the shellac finish, clean it with hand cleaner to guarantee that you will not be mixing dirt back into the finish when you amalgamate it.

Using Stain to Revive the Finish

There are two ways to revive a finish with stain. Use Minwax stain to revive finishes that have had sunlight or water damage. Bartley Gel Stain is the other stain I recommend. This is actually a finish with stain in it. It's good for reviving finishes that have become dull and lifeless.

REVIVING A FINISH USING MINWAX STAIN

This process will often work for areas damaged by water or sunlight. A good example would be the area beneath a kitchen sink that has become white and milky-looking due to water damage, or a chest of drawers that has had one side exposed to excessive sunlight, which also causes the finish to become white and milky-looking. Both sunlight and water affect the cycles of expansion and contraction within the finish and cause a shattering effect. Just as you cannot see through a shattered windshield, a shattered finish prevents you from seeing clearly through to the wood. Sunlight can also bleach the wood, making the exposed area lighter.

Supplies

One half-pint of Minwax stain in a color that matches that of the piece being worked on (Minwax stain works best for this job because of its thin consistency; it will penetrate better than heavy-bodied or gel-type stains)

Two clean cloths

The Process

Mix the stain thoroughly and apply with a clean cloth. You simply need to apply the stain and wipe it off. The stain won't work any better if you leave it on longer. This process will work on some finishes but not all. Some pieces that have heavier finishes, like the tops of tables and chests of drawers, will not accept the stain, but the stain won't harm such finishes. In fact, since the stain has a mineral spirit base, it will clean the finish as it adds color to it.

The above supplies cost less than $4.00. If you find this process doesn't work, the furniture suffers no adverse effects. Your only expense is the few dollars you spent for the stain and the trip to the hardware store. (And, of course, you will have to throw away the rag.)

The cabinets were in my house when I moved in, and I doubt any work had been done on them in twenty years. Despite years of neglect, they came to life in less than ten minutes and for less than $4.00.

At this point you will notice the areas that need to be touched up, and you may see paint specks or drips, dried milk (if you're working in the kitchen), and areas scratched through the finish that will need special attention.

A typical cabinet front might be beneath a sink, and you should expect to see water damage to the cabinet doors. This problem can be repaired for approximately $7.00, including cleaning the brasses. All of this can be done without removing any of the cabinet doors and without refinishing, and it should only take forty minutes to complete the entire job from start to finish. I should point out that this is typical damage to kitchen cabinet finishes due to water (high humidity). Many finishes damaged in this way can be repaired, but there are exceptions to this rule, depending on the finish and the type and severity of damage.

Reviving a Finish Using Bartley Gel Stain

The Bartley gel stain is a finish with a stain in it. I did a few minutes of preparation before applying it. Using 220 grit sandpaper, I sanded over the area shown simply to smooth it out and to sand off any loose finish. Once the area was smooth, I used a sponge brush and applied the stain.

Supplies

Bartley gel stain to match the original color

2-inch sponge brush

Clean cloth

The Process

The process is really very simple. Dip only the tip of the spongebrush in the stain, because this way you will be able to control the stain easily. Brush the stain on the wood, working with the grain. You can immediately begin gently wiping off the excess stain. After you have completely wiped off the stained area, you may need to go back and shade in certain areas to make the color uniform. This last light coat should not be wiped off.

Applying a New Finish Over Old Finish

Oily waxes and cleaners are an ineffective, quick-fix way to try to revive an old finish. They can damage the finish even further, because they often stay wet, attract dust, and contain who knows what harmful ingredients in the first place. Applying a new coat of finish will give new life to many older pieces. It will protect the wood and bond with the existing finish, while oily waxes and cleaners mixed with water can penetrate the finish and harm both it and the wood. Even if the oily wax or water doesn't harm the wood initially, the piece will need to be cleaned over and over again, until at some point it will do harm.

I will describe how to apply two types of finish over existing finish. One recommendation is that no matter which of these you use, you should prepare the piece of furniture before applying the finish. Do this by lightly sanding (220 grit or greater) the surface to be finished. This will facilitate bonding between the existing finish and the new finish you are applying. It is imperative that you sand very lightly, or you could sand through the finish and create additional problems. If you aren't confident about your sanding, you can use superfine steel wool, but it won't do the job as easily or quite as well.

The first finish we will discuss is shellac. Almost all furniture made prior to 1925 has shellac on it if it has not been refinished. An easy way to test and see if you're dealing with a shellac finish is to apply denatured alcohol to an inconspicuous area of the piece. The denatured alcohol will begin to dissolve shellac, but it will be harmless to other finishes.

Shellac can be purchased premixed or in flake form. Mixing your own shellac sounds much more intimidating than it is. Shellac solutions are measured in *cuts*, which denotes how many pounds of shellac are dissolved in one gallon of solvent. Thus, a gallon of "two pound cut shellac" contains two pounds of shellac in one gallon of solvent. If you want to finish a piece to a high gloss, I recommend Behlen's Super Blonde shellac, which has almost no wax and will provide great clarity down to the wood.

If the piece is to be sanded, especially if it is to be powersanded, I recommend using orange shellac (also called amber shellac), which has a higher wax content (4%). This wax will lubricate the surface and prevent it from becoming gummy as it is sanded.

One important thing to remember when mixing and applying shellac is that shellac works best in *thin* coats. The point is not to make a thick finish, just a beautiful one. Thus, I would not recommend making any shellac stronger than a two-pound cut.

Supplies

Half-pint of denatured alcohol

One pint of white shellac (which is actually clear)

3-inch sponge brush

The Process

It's important to clean the old finish before applying any sort of finish over another finish. (You may want to review the section on reviving a finish with hand cleaner earlier in this chapter.) After the finish is clean, it may be helpful to lightly sand or use superfine steel wool.

Applying shellac is really very simple, but remember that it dries quickly. Because your working time is limited, if you notice that you have missed a spot, it is better to let that area dry before going back over it. You can make a big mess if you try to touch it up while it's in the middle of drying. Use the denatured alcohol to thin the shellac if necessary. Then just brush on the shellac with the sponge brush in a thin, even coat. One coat may be all you need, but if you want to do a second, wait several hours before doing so.

The second finish I recommend you use is Bartley gel finish. This yields a finish that looks like hand-rubbed varnish and has the protective qualities of polyurethane. This finish is excellent to use on cabinet doors, especially those that aren't particularly old but have begun to show signs of wear. A good example would be the cabinet door below a sink.

Supplies

Bartley gel finish

3-inch sponge brush

Clean cloth

The Process

Bartley gel finish is a brush-on, wipe-off finish. It's best to work in small sections with the grain, brushing the finish on and then coming back over the section with a clean cloth to wipe off the finish. You should wipe the finish off immediately after applying it. Although the finish dries quickly, you should wait overnight before using the piece.

THE VICTROLA I RUINED

Reviving an old finish always reminds me of the Victrola I was given twenty years ago. Had I known of the above processes, this section would be headlined "The Victrola I Saved." It played just great, and I had lots of fun when my friends came over playing the old 78 rpm records on it. I hadn't had it long before deciding to work my magic and refinish it.

I took it out to the garage where I had done several other refinishing projects and took it apart. It wasn't long before I began to feel that I had started something I wished I hadn't. There were so many parts! I noticed as I stripped off the old finish that the "Victrola" decal also came off. I worked for a while longer and decided to finish the project in a few weeks. I was later transferred to another city and never finished the work because some of the parts were lost in the move. Ironically, I have a similar Victrola now. Its finish has been restored and it looks great. I did the work in my living room in about an hour.

The replacement for the Victrola I ruined.

SUMMARY: REVIVING OLD FINISHES

• Cleaning a lifeless finish with DL Blue Label Hand Cleaner and buffing with a soft cloth may be all that is needed to add new life and luster.

• Many finishes look in need of refinishing because there are many small damaged areas in the finish. Examples would be the cabinet door below your sink that has small milky white lines in it or a table or chair leg with numerous nicks and scratches. Wiping Minwax stain that matches the color of the piece over these areas will most often penetrate the small damaged areas and restore the appearance of the piece.

• Reviving old finishes with solvents is often difficult. A test should be made in an inconspicuous area first.

• Applying a new finish over an old finish may be a good idea, especially for the doors below the sink on your kitchen cabinets if they are showing signs of finish deterioration. Regardless, before you apply a new finish to your chest of drawers, it may be a good idea to test an area first.

4.
Touch-Ups

Whenever I hold a class or seminar on furniture, one of the fun things to do is to demonstrate how to do touch-ups. I will carry along a chair or other small piece to work on. This is what I will ask: "What needs to be done to restore this piece and how long will it take?" Then we talk about what supplies will be needed. If a professional did the work, how much would it cost? Here's where the real fun comes in.

After getting suggestions about stripping or sanding and how long it will take and how much money it will cost, I will state that the piece can be restored, while the class watches, for less than five dollars. At this point I will hear, "Yeah, sure," from the back of the room.

It is the minor flaws that can make a finish look really bad. We talked in the last chapter about how a dirty finish can look like a finish that needs to be redone. The minor nicks and scratches can give a bad appearance to a finish, and to the untrained eye the piece might seem to need refinishing. But, in fact, a few minor touch-ups can restore the piece to nearly its original beauty.

I'm sure at some point you've walked into an office and seen a beautiful desk with rubs and scratches around the baseboard, which really detracted from the beauty of the piece. Most of these mars are caused by cleaning personnel hitting the desk with a vacuum cleaner, leaving a white rub mark. Another major cause of these can be from shoes hitting the baseboard, causing rub marks and scratches.

Always think of touch-ups as small damaged areas of the finish. The damaged area may be a nick or scratch, a cigarette burn or a white water ring. All of these will detract from the beauty of the finish.

RUB MARKS

Let's start with the simplest of these, which are white rub marks. We should first describe the problem, which is often a skid mark created by the rubber bumper on a vacuum. Sometimes these are black and sometimes they're white. The white marks are far more noticeable. This is what you will need to correct this problem.

Supplies
DL Blue Label Hand Cleaner
0000 steel wool
Clean cloth

The Process
The process is simple. Put a small amount of hand cleaner on a piece of steel wool and rub with the grain. Most often this is all that is required to remove these marks. In some cases, the wood will have been hit so hard that there is rubber left in the grain or forced into the wood. If this is the case (and you will find out quickly), you will need more supplies, which are:

Artist's brush

Can of Minwax stain (as close as possible to the color of the piece you are touching up)

Clean cloth

Apply the stain with the artist's brush, then wipe it off gently with a clean cloth. This may require several tries to get the color just right.

Note: I use Minwax stain one of three ways:

1. Unmixed, leaving the majority of the pigment on the bottom.
2. Reaching to the bottom of the can with a screwdriver to pick up settled pigment.
3. Mixed evenly.

Each of these methods will provide a different intensity of color. The method I choose depends on the color of the piece.

RUBBED-THROUGH EDGES

Another problem you can touch up is edges where the finish is rubbed through. For this you will need the following supplies.

Supplies

Permanent felt marker matching the finish color (hundreds of colors of markers are available at art supply stores)

If the permanent marker isn't available, use an artist's brush and Minwax stain that matches the color of the finish.

The Process

Lightly draw a line with the marker along the edge that is worn.

If you are using the Minwax stain, draw the line with the artist's brush.

NUMEROUS NICKS AND SCRATCHES

Supplies

Minwax stain

Several clean cloths

Artist's brush

Razor blade

The Process

First, put stain on a cloth and wipe it on the piece. After wiping the stain off, most of the nicks and scratches will disappear. Often there are specks of paint that will need to be removed. This can be done by gently moving the razor blade across the finish. Finally, you will need the artist's brush to stain any small spots that remain.

SCRATCHES ON TABLE TOPS

Scratches to table tops fall into four categories of severity. One is the scratch you can see but can't actually feel. The second is a scratch that's in the finish — you can just barely feel it with your fingernail. The third scratch is deeper into the finish but has not broken the surface of the wood, and you can feel it with your fingernail. The last and most severe is a scratch that goes through the finish to the wood or into the wood. This last one is the most noticeable because it has actually scratched the stain from the surface of the wood. We'll look at these in order from the easiest to touch up to the most difficult.

Repairing a Minor Scratch
Supplies

Water or vegetable oil

Rottenstone

Clean cloth

Paste wax

The Process

Rottenstone is available at most hardware stores. It can be applied either with a wet cloth or with a cloth that has oil on it. The vegetable oil you have in your kitchen will work fine for this job. Either way, dampen a cloth with water or vegetable oil and sprinkle a small amount of the rottenstone over the scratched area. With the cloth, rub in a circular motion to remove the scratch. It may be necessary to paste wax the table top to make the sheen uniform again.

Using the sanding block with 400 grit wet/dry sandpaper and water. Water keeps the finish cool, so the heat of friction will not damage it.

Repairing a Scratch that You Can Just Barely Feel with Your Fingernail

Supplies

1 sheet 600 grit wet/dry sandpaper

Small dry sponge

Vegetable oil or water

Rottenstone

Clean cloth

Paste wax

The Process

Cut the sheet of wet/dry sandpaper in strips so that each piece is about ½ inch wider than the small dry sponge. Apply 1 tablespoon of oil or water to the scratched area. Wrap the wet/dry sandpaper around the end of the dry sponge. (It may be best to put the dry sponge in a plastic sandwich bag to keep it from absorbing water or oil, as you will be using this as a sanding block.) With the sponge and sandpaper, sand over the scratch, being careful not to sand through the finish. Make several passes with the sandpaper and check to see if the scratch is gone. If not, continue sanding carefully.

When the scratch is removed, the sheen will need to be rubbed to match the rest of the table. This can be done as described earlier.

Repairing a Scratch Deep into the Finish that Has Not Broken Through to the Wood

The process described here is called a *burn-in*. This is a difficult process that requires lots of experience, but it is the only way to repair this type of scratch and should only be done by someone who has experience using the burn-in process.

Supplies

Mineral spirits

Clean cloths

Clear shellac stick

Burn-in knife

Burn-in balm

Rubbing oil

600 grit wet/dry sandpaper

Sanding block

Rubbing compound

French finish

First, use mineral spirits on a cloth to remove the wax from the area to be repaired. Heat the shellac stick with the burn-in knife, allowing the melted shellac to flow into the scratch so that there is enough material in the scratch to bring it above the level of the surrounding finish. As the melted shellac cools and rehardens, press it down with your thumb to make sure it is packed into the scratch. When hardened, apply a liberal amount of burn-in balm over and around the scratch. This will serve two purposes: (1) the burn-in balm will make the burn-in easier to work; and (2) it will prevent the shellac from adhering to adjacent areas of the finish when heated and leveled.

LEVELING THE BURN-IN

The burn-in is leveled by gently making passes across the top of the burn-in with the hot knife to slowly remelt the shellac. Passes are made as an airplane would make touch-and-go landings. The knife comes down easily across the burn-in and is lifted again. With each succeeding pass, the pressure is increased upon the melting shellac to the point that the blade of the knife will draw flat across the existing finish. Stop with the knife and allow several minutes for the shellac to reharden. Clean the area with a dry cloth to remove the burn-in balm, which may still remain on the surface.

SANDING THE BURN-IN

Sanding the burn-in should be done with 600 grit wet/dry sandpaper on a sanding block, using rubbing oil as the lubricant. This will completely level the burn-in with the existing finish. After sanding, wipe the table off with a clean, dry cloth.

REPLACING THE SHEEN

In some cases, the sheen can be replaced by simply using a rubbing compound and then waxing. Often it requires padding the area with French finish, which is described in Chapter 6.

CIGARETTE BURNS

The method for repair of cigarette burns depends on the depth of the burn. Often the burn is only in the finish and does not go into the wood. If this is the case, scrape away the burned finish with a pocket knife. Using an artist's brush, apply fast-drying varnish-based sanding sealer. Apply several coats and allow them to dry in order to fill the depression. Sand the area with 600 grit wet/dry sandpaper to level it.

The finish I recommend for a touch-up like this is Bartley clear gel finish. The Bartley clear gel finish will do the job in most cases, but if the finish has a high gloss, the burned area should be finished over by French padding. (For instructions on French padding, see Chapter 6.)

Burns that penetrate the wood cannot be dealt with using this method. Burn-ins, discussed in Chapter 4, are the best way to fix burns into the wood.

CLOUDS IN THE FINISH

Moisture trapped in a finish can create white clouds. There are several methods for removing these blemishes. The success you have in removing them will depend on how deep into the finish the cloud is set. Heat may cause a fast evaporation of the moisture within the wood, thus creating a white cloud deep in the finish. Water works the other way. Moisture can condense on the finish from a water glass or vase and work its way into the finish. Clouds caused by water tend to be nearer the surface and are thus easier to remove. Again, this depends on the depth of the cloud.

I recently spent the morning at Ash Lawn repairing just such a problem caused by a vase on a tabletop. I first cleaned the tabletop with fine steel wool and DL Blue Label Hand Cleaner. Then I wiped the table down with a clean cloth and waxed it using Goddard's paste wax and more fine steel wool, spending extra time on the white spot. I removed the white spot using the paste wax and fine steel wool because this was a surface cloud. The paste wax and steel wool work similarly to a rubbing compound and will very lightly cut down the finish. What I then did was to use a clean piece of steel wool to go over the whole table, working with the grain. I then buffed it with a clean cloth.

For a deeper white spot, steel wool and paste wax won't get far enough into the finish. Instead, use mineral oil and a cotton swab or cotton balls. Take the cotton swab and put two or three drops of oil on it. Work the cotton into the finish in a small circle over the white spot. This motion will create a small amount of heat and force the mineral oil into the finish. This tends to darken the area somewhat, but the white spot will be less noticeable like this than it was before you applied the oil.

PRESS MARKS

A press mark is a flaw in the finish that has been caused by pressure on the finish. Such flaws often occur when furniture is shipped and padding is used to protect it. Press marks can also result from consistent pressure applied on the finish over time, like that applied by a lamp placed on an end table. The easiest way to deal with press marks is to apply paste wax using steel wool. Use a fair amount of pressure on the steel wool and paste wax, because otherwise you will be simply waxing the finish. To unite the sheen, wax the whole top once the pressmark has been eradicated.

SUMMARY: TOUCH-UPS

- Remedy white rub marks with hand cleaner and steel wool. For more stubborn marks, try Minwax stain.

- Help rubbed-through edges with permanent felt marker that matches the finish color, or with Minwax stain.

- For numerous nicks and scratches, wipe on Minwax stain with a soft cloth.

- Repair a minor scratch with rottenstone applied with either a wet cloth or a cloth dampened with vegetable oil.

- To remedy a shallow cigarette burn, scrape out the burned area with a pocket knife and apply sanding sealer.

- Press marks can be touched up with paste wax applied using steel wool.

5.
Repairs

It seems that every week someone will bring a chair or another piece to the shop that has broken or come loose and an attempt has been made to repair the piece at home. Often the loose parts will be coated with glue, which of course must be removed before a repair can be made properly. Then there are the minor repairs that have turned into major repairs because they have been ignored for so long that finally a leg or back breaks. These cost much more to fix as it is necessary to repair broken parts rather than simply fix loose parts.

Over the last twenty-two years I have probably tried every type of glue I could get my hands on to do repairs. It wasn't until I had a job repairing 120 chairs in a restaurant that I discovered Devcon 5-Minute Epoxy, a two-part epoxy that can be purchased at most hardware stores for about $3.00. It comes in a syringe tube and is easy to use. When I began to use Devcon Epoxy, a whole new world of repair processes and techniques opened up to me.

USING EPOXY

Learning to use epoxy completely revolutionized my approach to doing repairs. Instead of waiting all day or even overnight for glue to dry, I could now use epoxy to do a repair and have a stronger, cleaner repair in about ten minutes. I like repairing furniture, and learning how to use epoxy has added to the enjoyment and the profits I make from doing durable repairs.

Epoxy and white glue are the two primary glues I use to do repairs in my shop. Here are a few tips on using epoxy.

- Double check to make sure the parts you are gluing fit together properly before applying the epoxy.
- The epoxy is dispensed from the tube in two parts and must be mixed thoroughly or it will never dry and harden.
- Apply the epoxy to the loose parts and press them together. The epoxy will begin to harden after a few minutes, and at this point you should peel off the excess with your fingernail.
- Let the repair dry (fifteen minutes or so) and you're finished.

Epoxy is far superior to white glue for many repairs. We still often use white glue, but it requires clamping.

I will be describing various repairs below, some of which you may want to try and some you might rather leave to a professional. This is by no means an exhaustive list of all possible repairs; rather it is a brief list of general repairs you are likely to come across.

CHAIR REPAIRS

Among the possible chair repairs you will run into are:

- loose spreader
- broken spreader
- broken chair back
- broken spindle
- loose chair seat

LOOSE SPREADER

Supplies

Devcon 5-Minute Epoxy

Something to mix the epoxy on (a small piece of cardboard works well)

Something to mix the epoxy with (a screwdriver or pocket knife works well)

The Process

First, make sure that the loose spreader is not caked with glue. If it is, you will have to sand or scrape off the old glue. Once any old glue has been removed, make sure the parts fit together properly. Before applying new glue, put the spreader back between the legs and fit it in place. If it doesn't fit, it's possible more glue needs to be removed. When the parts fit together properly, loosen them and mix the epoxy. Remember, it's important that you mix the epoxy thoroughly, or it will not dry properly. Apply a generous amount of epoxy around the loose spreader, and join it back together with the leg. It may be necessary to hold the chair leg for a few minutes if the spreader won't stay in place by itself until the epoxy begins to set. You can tell when the epoxy has begun to set because it will become rubbery. When it does, you should remove any excess epoxy from around the spreader and from any tools you have been using.

If there are several loose spreaders on the chair, I generally repair them one or two at a time, rather than try to do them all at once, as time is limited using the two-part quick-setting epoxy. Again, make sure the parts fit together properly before you mix the epoxy and that you mix the epoxy thoroughly. You should be able to do this type of repair without clamps or any other tools.

BROKEN SPREADER

Instead of replacing broken spreaders, I've found that I can repair them and make the repaired area stronger than it was originally. This has worked particularly well for spreaders that would have had to be turned on a lathe and stained and matched to the original. Turning a spreader is a time-consum-

ing process in itself, and often makes the repair so expensive that it's simply not justifiable. With this repair, you can rescue chairs you might otherwise have discarded.

There are two ways spreaders can break. They either break horizontally along the grain or vertically across the grain. The first of these is easier to repair and will be discussed first.

Supplies

Devcon 5-Minute Epoxy

Screwdriver to apply and mix the epoxy

Pocket knife

2 C-clamps

The Process

When a spreader breaks along the grain, it provides a long surface on which to apply epoxy. After thoroughly mixing the epoxy, use the screwdriver to apply the epoxy all along the break. Place one C-clamp at each end of the break. Begin by applying gentle pressure on each end of the break and gradually tighten the clamps alternately. After the epoxy has begun to cure, gently carve it down with the pocket knife. No touching up should be required.

Repairing a spreader with a vertical break is more involved, but this is still an easy repair. Before we start, let me give you the gist of what will follow. First, the epoxy dries very hard and is very strong. By drilling a hole into each end of the spreader, we will place a short steel rod to join the two broken pieces that will float in the hole. Space around the rod will be filled with epoxy and become very strong.

Supplies

Drill

Drill bit approximately $1/2$ the width of the spreader

Devcon 5-Minute Epoxy

Screwdriver to mix the epoxy

Steel rod about $1/3$ the width of the spreader (this could be a large nail with the head cut off)

Wax paper

The Process

Remove the two pieces of the spreader from the chair. Do this by gently working each glue joint loose. Drill a hole about 1 inch deep in each end of the spreader where it is broken. Try to center the holes with your eye, but the two holes do not have to match up exactly. Place the steel rod in one of the holes and attempt to fit the two pieces together. Make any adjustments to the holes at this point so that the steel rod will fit, because the epoxy dries quickly once it has been mixed. Once the pieces fit together comfortably, mix up enough epoxy to fill the space around the steel rod. Put epoxy in both holes, slide the steel rod in one of them, and push the two spreaders together so the break matches up. Set the repaired spreader on the wax paper and simply hold it together for several minutes. Before the epoxy has completely cured, remove any excess epoxy with your fingernail. You can leave it on the wax paper to cure, because the glue will not stick to the wax paper.

It is possible to do this same repair with the spreader still in the chair, but the holes in the ends of the spreader are a little more difficult to drill. Often spreaders will break off flush with a leg of the chair. Repair this type of break just as described above, but understand that breaks flush with a leg must be done in place.

Broken Chair Arm

Often customers who call me about repairs to chairs or rocking chairs believe a new part will be necessary to fix the chair. In fact, many of these broken parts can be repaired rather than replaced and actually be made stronger than new. In the example shown, the customer brought this chair into my shop, believing a new arm would have to be made. He was concerned that it would be so expensive it wouldn't be worth fixing the chair. This repair is similar to the one above for repairing a spreader with a vertical break.

Supplies

Devcon 5-Minute Epoxy

3-inch steel rod (³/₈ inch thick)

Drill

⁷/₁₆-inch drill bit

Pocket knife with a sharp blade

120 grit sandpaper

220 grit sandpaper

¹/₂-inch wood chisel

Heavy-bodied stain to match the chair

Masking tape

3-inch sponge brush

The Process

First, epoxy back any loose parts and also apply epoxy to the break in the arm, simply to hold it together while completing the repair. Mark off ¹/₂ inch from the end of the drill bit and place a piece of tape around the bit to ensure that each hole is the same depth. Use the ⁷/₁₆-inch drill bit to drill a series of holes in a straight line, forming a crater in the back of the chair in which you can place a steel rod. (It may be necessary to use the ¹/₂-inch wood chisel to straighten out the inside of the hole to fit the steel rod.) I use a steel rod in lieu of a wooden dowel for the strength of the steel. Test-fit the steel rod into the hole and remove. The rod should be at least ¹/₄ inch lower than the surface of the wood. At this point, the chair should be placed so that the steel rod is parallel to the floor so that the epoxy will not run off.

After removing the rod, fill the crater approximately ¹/₃ full with mixed epoxy and reinstall the bar, tapping it in if necessary to ensure that it is below the surface of the wood. Fill the rest of the crater with epoxy, so that the epoxy is slightly above the level of the wood. As the epoxy cures, it will become rubbery. To see if the epoxy has reached this stage, check the texture of the epoxy remaining on the surface where you mixed it and not on the repair. If it has a rubbery texture, now is the time to gently carve it down even with the wood on the back of the chair, using the pocket knife. Then leave the epoxy to cure. After the epoxy that holds the steel rod cures, sand it down even with the chair back. Use the 120 grit sandpaper first, taking care not to sand over the wooden area, if possible. The final sanding should be done with 220 grit sandpaper.

Color the repaired area to match the existing wood, applying the stain lightly with the sponge brush.

BROKEN CHAIR SPINDLE

Spindles may look fragile, but they can be repaired successfully in a similar fashion to the process above for repairing broken spreaders. One difference is that you should not remove the spindle, repair it, and try to replace it, because sometimes you won't be able to get it back in without removing the back of the chair.

There are three general ways spindles can break. They may break off flush at either end. They can also break vertically along the grain of the wood, and the final (and most involved) break is one across the grain horizontally.

If the spindle is broken off flush you will need:

Supplies

Devcon 5-Minute Epoxy

Drill

Small drill bit (approximately $1/32$ inch)

Hammer

$3/4$-inch finish nail or brad

Countersink punch

The Process

First, apply epoxy to the spindle at the break, simply to hold it in place while you complete the repair. When the glue holding the spindle in place has dried, use a small drill bit ($1/32$ inch) to drill a hole at an angle through the broken spindle into the top of the chair. Cut the head off a small finishing nail and gently drive the finishing nail into the hole you have drilled. Countersink the nail with a countersink punch in order to hide it. Fill the small hole left behind with a crayon filler, which is a wax-type stick available at hardware stores. It comes in different colors.

For a spindle with a vertical break you will need:

Supplies

Devcon 5-Minute Epoxy

Pocket knife

2 C-clamps

The Process

This repair is very much the same as that previously described for a spreader with a horizontal break. Apply epoxy to the break. It is best to use two small C-clamps, one at each end of the break, tightened to a snug fit.

For a spindle with a horizontal break you will need:

Supplies

Drill

Drill bit approximately half the width of the spindle

Devcon 5-Minute Epoxy

Screwdriver to mix the epoxy

Steel rod about $1/3$ the width of the spindle (this could be a nail with the head cut off)

The Process

As with repairing spreaders, use a drill bit that is approximately half the width of the spindle. If the spindle is small with a vertical break in it, you're going to have to use a small drill bit. Careful drilling by sight is necessary.

This is much the same as repairing a spreader with a vertical break, but you may find that the spindle needs to be repaired in place, as opposed to removing it, because you may not be able to get it back in. Don't use too long a rod or nail for this type of repair, because you might not be able to move the two parts of the spindle enough to fit the rod or nail in the two holes.

As with all repairs using epoxy, make a test run before mixing the epoxy to be sure the parts will fit together. After drilling the two holes, test the fit by placing the nail in the bottom part of the spindle. Push both parts of the spindle backwards until the nail can slide easily into the top half. Then simply repeat the process, but this time fill each hole about half full of epoxy, making sure to work some epoxy up into the top hole.

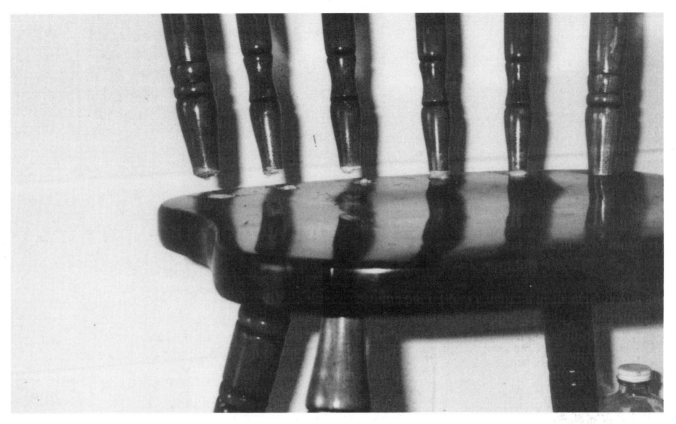

If the owner hadn't waited so long to repair the chair, the repair could have been simple and inexpensive. Now the chair has four broken spindles.

This small broken spindle is simple to repair and will be stronger after the repair.

A hole is drilled into each end of the spindle, slightly larger than the steel pin that will be inserted.

The pin is test-fit in the two holes before applying epoxy. This ensures a snug fit.

The pieces are epoxied together.

A broken spindle.

Use two C-clamps for equal pressure while the epoxy dries. If you use only one clamp, the piece will slip one way or another.

LOOSE CHAIR SEAT

Supplies

Devcon 5-Minute Epoxy

Screwdriver

Rubber hammer

Bar clamp

The Process

The first thing to do is remove the seat. Most times this will involve turning the chair upside down and removing the four screws holding the seat in place. Second, remove the two corner blocks that secure the seat runner to the back. Often these are glued and screwed into the chair. If the seat is loose, one or more of these glue joints is probably broken. Thus, after removing the screws, if the piece does not come out readily, you will have to tap it loose to break the remaining glue bond. Use the rubber hammer to separate the leg from the rail. Adjust the bar clamp so it will be ready to use and make a dry run to guarantee that the parts will fit properly. Apply the Devcon 5-Minute Epoxy around the exposed dowels and to the end of the rail. Position the bar clamp to ensure that it is parallel to the rail, and tighten it. If the bar clamp is not parallel with the rail, the chair may rack itself; that is to say, one or more of the chair legs will not meet the floor.

CHEST OF DRAWERS REPAIRS

Many of these repairs will require new pieces. If you have access to a table saw, you can cut the pieces yourself. If not, many lumber supply companies would be able to cut pieces of the appropriate size for you. All you would have to do is provide them with the measurements of the piece you need. Pine wood is fine for these small pieces.

DRAWER STOPS

The function of the drawer stop is to stop the drawer even with the front of the chest. It can either be located at the back of the chest or on the front frame of the chest so that the drawer face meets it to stop the drawer. Each drawer will have two drawer stops. If the drawer stop is missing on one side, the drawer may go in too far on that side; if both stops are missing, the drawer will go in too far on both sides. If you remove the drawer it should be obvious where the missing drawer stops were located.

Supplies

Small block of wood (approximately 1/4 inch thick, 1 1/2 inch long, and 1 inch wide)

Coping saw

1/2-inch nails

Tack hammer

Wood glue

Ruler

The Process

The easiest way to get a wood block of the size described is at a building supply store. They sell wooden screen door molding, which would be fine for this job. It may be necessary to buy an 8' length of it, but it should only cost you about a dollar. If the stop is located on the front frame of the chest, simply measure the depth of the facing of the drawer and place the wood block that distance back from the edge of the frame. Apply glue to the bottom of the block and set it in place. Then put one nail through the block to hold it in place.

On some chests of drawers, the drawer stops are placed at the back of the drawer glide. To repair these stops, place the small block of wood at the end of the drawer glide. Then slide the drawer back into place. At this point, the drawer will either go too far or not far enough. It may be best to use a strip of wood that is a little longer than you think is necessary so that it can be cut shorter. Once the drawer stops in the proper position, you can glue and nail the drawer stop in place.

DRAWER GLIDES

Drawer glides are located both on the drawer and within the chest. These are what the drawer glides on as it is moved in and out of the chest. These are commonly damaged, but as mentioned in Chapter 2, occasional waxing will help keep them in good condition. Removal of the drawer will make it very easy to inspect the drawer glides within the chest

A worn drawer glide needs to be replaced. This kind of wear can be prevented by waxing the drawer glide every two or three years or whenever it begins to stick.

and the glides on the bottom of the drawer. If the drawer glide within the chest is worn excessively, it is often possible to remove it, turn it over, and glue it back into position. This will also require removing the drawer guide and repositioning it on top of the glide.

The easiest way to get a piece of wood to use as a new drawer glide is to call your local lumberyard and give them the dimensions of the piece you need. This is especially true if you don't have a table saw to cut the glides with.

MISSING OR BADLY WORN DRAWER GLIDE
If your drawer falls down in the back when you push it into the chest, then the drawer glide is either missing or severely worn.

Supplies
Ruler

White glue

Wood cut to specifications

³/₄-inch finishing nails

Hammer

The Process
Remove the guide from the top of the glide. Installation of the new glide should be very simple. It's a matter of applying glue to the side of the glide that goes up against the chest of drawers and setting it in place. Use one of the ³/₄-inch finishing nails at the front of the glide and one at the back of the glide, hammering them in at a 45 degree angle.

LOOSE DRAWER GLIDE
Often drawer glides become loose and cause the drawer to fall down as it is slid into place. This repair is simple and should require only a little glue and one nail.

Supplies

White glue

3/4-inch finishing nails

Hammer

The Process

This repair is done just like the previous repair for a missing drawer glide. You should put one nail at the front and one at the back of the drawer glide at a 45 degree angle. They will hold the glide in place until the glue dries, because you will not really be able to use a clamp in this situation. Hammer the nails all the way in, however, because you don't need to worry about taking them out after the glue has dried.

MISSING DRAWER GUIDE

The purpose of the drawer guide is to guide the drawer into and out of the chest. It keeps the drawer moving straight in and out. Here is a test to tell if a drawer guide is missing or loose: you should be able to put your hand on either side of the drawer and push it in. It should stay in line with the opening in the chest.

Again, the easiest way to find a piece of wood to use for a drawer guide is to call a local lumberyard and give them the dimensions of the piece you need.

Supplies

Ruler

Wood cut to proper dimensions

Wood glue

1-inch finishing nails

Hammer

The Process

Glue the drawer guide to the top of the drawer glide, making sure to leave enough room for the drawer to slide into place. Nail a finishing nail straight down at both the front and back of the guide.

LOOSE DRAWER GUIDE

Supplies

Wood glue

1-inch finishing nail

Hammer

The Process

If the drawer guide is loose, it will be easy to remove. Once you have removed it, it will most likely have two nails in it, which held it in place. All you need to do is put some glue on the bottom of the guide and put the two original nails back in their original holes. Depending on how tightly the nails fit in their original holes, you may want to put in a third nail for additional strength.

DRAWER REPAIRS

MISSING OR DAMAGED DRAWER GLIDES

One of the most common repairs needed to drawers is worn or missing drawer glides. These can be easily repaired, but it will require measuring the missing part. You will need to measure its depth as well as its length and width. Often when a drawer glide breaks off, it is necessary to square off the bottom of the drawer with a wood chisel to facilitate placement of the new drawer glide.

Supplies

Drawer glide (cut to specifications)

Chisel

Five-minute Devcon 5-Minute Epoxy

The Process

After chiseling the bottom of the drawer flat to make it easier to place the drawer glide, mix Devcon 5-Minute Epoxy and use it to glue the new drawer glide to the bottom of the drawer. It's best not to use finishing nails or nails of any type on a drawer glide because as the drawer glide begins to wear, the nails will be exposed and will damage the drawer glide on the inside of the piece of furniture.

LOOSE DRAWER PARTS

This process is a repair suitable for drawers that have become loose at their joints and are beginning to fall apart. Gluing the parts together is a simple process, but what is important is that you put the drawer back together square at its joints. Use Devcon 5-Minute Epoxy for these repairs, because if you were to use wood glue or white glue, you would have to clamp the parts together. Make sure parts fit together properly and are square before you apply epoxy.

BROKEN BEDPOSTS

The process of repairing a broken bedpost is very similar to the process described above for broken chair spreaders and spindles. Again, we will be inserting a steel rod for increased strength at the break.

There are two main advantages to using this method to repair a broken bedpost. First, the break will be stronger than before it was broken. Second, the epoxy will fill any gap between the steel rod and the wood, meaning that the holes don't have to be perfectly aligned and can be drilled somewhat larger than the steel rod.

Supplies

Drill

$5/8$-inch wood drill bit

3-inch piece of $1/2$-inch steel rod

Five minute Devcon 5-Minute Epoxy

The Process

Using the drill and the wood drill bit, drill a hole as close to center as possible in each end of the break. Test fit the steel rod. If the steel rod will not fit, reinsert the drill bit into either hole and in a circular motion increase the size of the hole in one end of the break. Now test fit the steel rod again. Once the rod fits appropriately, mix a small amount of Devcon 5-Minute Epoxy and carefully put epoxy into the bottom hole so that the steel rod can be inserted into the hole without epoxy overflowing. Put the top

piece back on and allow the steel rod to set. When it is set (approximately five minutes), remove the top portion of the break. Mix Devcon 5-Minute Epoxy and put a small amount in the hole of the top piece. Apply epoxy to the break itself also. Put the two parts back together, carefully fitting the edges of the break together. You may want to tap the top of the bedpost with a rubber mallet to ensure a close fit. Before the epoxy sets, make sure the bedpost is straight.

As the epoxy dries, it will become rubbery. This is the time to remove excess epoxy with your fingernail. Support the bedpost in its proper position until the epoxy has cured. It may be necessary to touch up the break with a matching stain to complete the repair.

SUMMARY: REPAIRS

- Learn to use epoxy — you can have clean, strong repairs in minutes.
- Repair a loose chair spreader with epoxy.
- Broken spreaders should be drilled to accept a steel rod with epoxy to cement it in place.
- A broken chair spindle can be repaired in a similar fashion to a broken spreader.
- A loose chair seat can be screwed in place and epoxied for permanent strength.
- Loose or missing drawer glides, stops, and guides can easily be cut from new stock and glued/nailed in place.
- Broken bedposts can be repaired as described for broken chair spreaders.

6.
Refinishing

The furniture I refinished as a hobby and used in my home brought me a sense of satisfaction and pride. My friends would come to visit and comment on furniture I had refinished and want to know how much I paid for it or where I bought it. It was fun to reply that I paid ten dollars for the piece and refinished it myself. It wasn't long before I had a house full of furniture I had refinished. I began to get the feeling that I would just love to be in the furniture refinishing business. And that's just what I did. I rented a small space and started my business.

I look back to those days with a chuckle. Other friends who have gone into business for themselves relate the same experience, that they also grew in knowledge and expertise over the years. I thought I knew so much about furniture refinishing back then. I did know the basics of how to refinish a piece, but found out quickly that there were many new things to learn. Some pieces were easy to strip and finish; others presented a challenge. The easy pieces were oak, made during the Golden Oak Era (1880-1910). It was easy to strip off the old shellac that had become very dark and often alligatored. Stripped with patience and detail, it was then simply a matter of a light sanding and brushing on several coats of polyurethane. I learned quickly that stripping was very important to each of the refinishing steps to follow.

There were the other pieces that were as easy to strip as the oak but did not look as good when I worked my "magic." My "magic" had somehow lost its touch when it came to refinishing some veneered pieces. My early approach was to strip the piece and not stain it so as to see the "natural beauty of the wood." This worked just fine when I was refinishing oak or walnut, but when I was introduced to veneered pieces the "natural beauty of the wood" looked neither natural nor beautiful. As an example, I refinished a mahogany-veneered table with legs constructed of poplar. The mahogany veneer looked great, but the poplar legs were a light reddish color that looked really unnatural. What I missed was that the legs and edges of the top should have been stained so that the eye would be drawn to the mahogany veneer rather than the poplar. The top of the table looked good, but the light color of the legs made the table as a whole look bad. If a piece is constructed of different types of wood, each type of wood will require different treatment to result in a consistent look for the whole piece.

THE NATURAL BEAUTY OF THE WOOD

I would love to have a nickel for every time I've heard, "I would like to see the natural beauty of the wood." This would often be said when I looked at a piece of furniture to be refinished, and the customer would state that he did not want the piece stained. I felt the same way in my early days of refinishing, but as I learned with the mahogany-veneered table, this approach would work well for some pieces being refinished but for others it would not.

First, when removing the finish from a piece, much of the original stain that has penetrated the wood fibers will remain. Therefore, the appearance of the wood is not the natural color; rather it is the color of the stain that has been applied previously.

It is true that some woods have natural beauty (walnut, cherry, and mahogany, to name just a few) but others used to construct furniture do not. Maple, ash, oak, and poplar, among others, do not have much richness or contrast in the grain if not enhanced with stain. Sometimes the "natural beauty" of the wood is ugly next to the beauty of properly applied stain and finish.

STRIPPING BASICS

I can't imagine how many hours I would have saved and how much easier stripping would have been if I had had a better understanding of the stripping process ten years ago. I suppose I knew that stripping was the dirtiest and hardest part of the refinishing job, and I continually looked for a quick fix answer. The fact is that there is no quick fix for stripping. It will always be the hardest part of refinishing. The solution is simply to use enough paint remover to react with the old finish and remove it gently. Stripping is the first step in refinishing and often the most important step. My final words of advice about stripping are that the extra time you spend doing a really thorough job of stripping a piece — checking details, intricate areas — can save you a lot of problems in later steps.

It's important to emphasize that there is no quick fix for stripping a piece. The dip tanks and and water wash paint removers most often cause damage. The time saved in the quick stripping process is all lost in the extra work that will be required in later refinishing steps. It's the *reaction* of the paint remover with the old finish that is most important. Most furniture finishes are made of paint-related materials and are best removed using paint remover.

When I think of stripping, I remember the Hoosier Cabinet I refinished back in 1972. It had been painted with several coats of white paint. I knew that underneath was oak wood that would look great refinished. I couldn't wait to begin this refinishing

project and made a trip to the hardware store to buy the supplies to do the job.

Stripping off all that white paint became a real chore, and it was depressing as I felt I had begun a project that was taking so much time to strip. I suppose hindsight is 20-20, as I would certainly be able to do the stripping much more quickly now. After several months, my old cabinet was finally stripped of all the white paint and the finish underneath the paint. From that point on, finishing my project was a breeze.

I've never forgotten how bogged down I got with that project just doing the stripping. It changed my approach to doing future projects as I knew that painted pieces would take longer to complete, especially if there were many parts to deal with. I was also new to using paint remover and didn't give it enough time to work properly.

It didn't take long to realize that the hardest part was stripping. Of all the steps to refinish a piece — stripping, sanding, staining, and finishing — stripping took the most time. I read books and tried all sorts of methods to make the job of stripping easier.

My worst experience was stripping a painted oak chest with lye and water. Lye is extremely caustic. I feared that if one drop were to get on my skin it would burn a hole in me. The lye and water reacted with the wood and turned it very dark. The project was a disaster from start to finish. I would never again use this quick-fix method of removing the paint (which I had read about in some book) to ruin a piece of furniture.

Refinishing furniture is a gentle process, whereby the existing finish is removed and a new one applied. In this process, often the color of the stain, on or in the wood, is affected so that the wood will require staining to match the original color. It is possible to omit staining if the wood color is desirable after the old finish has been removed.

Remember, stripping is a gentle process to remove the old finish. Would you consider putting your favorite chest of drawers in a tank of lye and water and letting it remain there for an hour or so to

Saved from the stripper! This piece was restored for less than $10. Both the finish and the brasses were cleaned with hand cleaner.

remove the finish? Then, to make matters worse, would you wash it down with a high-powered water hose, the same kind you may have used at the car wash? If high humidity will harm your furniture, imagine what this will do. Two hours soaking in a tank! A radical way to remove the finish. It's quick and effective, a very effective way to remove a finish. The result is a damaging, harmful, unnecessary disaster for the wood, glue joints, and often veneer, on what may have been a cherished piece of your furniture. Need I say more? If you take your furniture for professional restoration, make sure it will not be dipped.

Enough about the wrong way to strip your furniture. Let's begin by defining refinishing. Refinishing is removing the old worn-out finish and replacing it with a new one. Think of it as replacing the picture window in your living room, which had become worn to the point that you could no longer see through it clearly. I think it's important to remember that stripping is a gentle process by which the old finish is removed. Unnecessary damage can be done to the wood and to irreplaceable patinas by harsh stripping and scraping of the wood. In most cases, the piece will require less sanding if it is stripped properly. Often older pieces will retain much of their value and character when proper stripping methods are used.

Enough Paint Remover and Enough Time

Two important factors will make a stripping project much, much easier. First, simply use enough paint remover for a reaction to occur between the paint remover and the old finish. Second, you must allow enough time for a reaction to occur. This may involve brushing on additional paint remover as the old finish absorbs the first coat. Paint remover can remove any type of furniture finish, since most of the finishes you will be dealing with are paint-related. These include shellac, varnish, and lacquer. Whether the finish is oil, varnish, a pigmented paint, or something else, all of these types of finishes go on wet and penetrate the wood fibers to some degree. Clear finishes are easier to strip by virtue of their inherent clarity; they will not affect

the color of the wood, nor will they be as noticeable in the grain of the wood as pigmented finishes are.

I have to reiterate that the best way to ease the job of stripping is to use enough paint remover and allow enough time for a reaction to occur. Think of it as trying to clean a dirty window without using enough window cleaner.

The Preparation

If you have any structural repairs to do to the piece, do them before you strip it. There are several reasons for this. First, the glue used in the repairs will work better if stripper doesn't get all over the wood to be glued. Second, you won't need to worry about damaging a finished area while you do the repair. A repaired area will blend in better if it is refinished along with the rest of the piece. Otherwise, it may require disturbing the stain or the finish in order to do a repair, which would be a headache. Other repairs, such as holes that need to be filled, chips in the wood, and other surface damage, should be done after the piece is stripped but before it is stained.

When preparing to strip a piece of furniture, consider the following:

1. Work in a well-ventilated space.

2. Be as comfortable as possible while you work. One suggestion is to have the piece you are stripping resting on a bench of sorts, so you can be seated on a stool. I find it very satisfying to listen to music while I work.

3. Prepare yourself mentally to take your time, allow enough time for proper reaction of the paint remover with the old finish (this may be several minutes), and do the detail work (e.g., make sure the corners are clean, the piece is wiped down with the grain properly, etc.). The minor detail work you do now will save many, many headaches later.

Applying and Using Paint Remover

Applying paint remover should be done with care. This is one of the first items I discuss with new employees who come to work for me. Here's why: Several years ago an employee was stripping the top

Supplies for stripping: fan for ventilation, plastic jug for paint remover, liquid paint remover, 3-inch brush, brush with bristles cut off to 1 inch, scraper (for heavier finishes or paint), rubber gloves, and rags.

Applying paint remover to a piece laid horizontally to hold the paint remover on the surface.

of a chest of drawers. While applying the paint remover, one drip flew off the brush, went across the room, and landed on top of a mahogany drop-leaf table that had just been buffed and was ready to deliver to a customer. To make matters worse, someone in the shop saw the drip of paint remover on the table and tried to wipe it off. The table could not be delivered until days later because of one drip of paint remover and the work required to repair the spot.

The drop of paint remover went flying across the room because the person doing the stripping allowed the brush to "flick" at the end of its movement across the table. I now teach every new employee to make a deliberate effort to stop the brush at the end of each pass and *slowly* turn it, rather than allow it to flick paint remover across the room and possibly onto another piece of furniture.

Applying the paint remover requires a light movement of the brush to leave as much material on the surface as possible. Heavier brushing leaves a lighter coat of paint remover and thus the amount of material left on the surface of the old finish will not be enough to create the necessary reaction of the paint remover with the old finish.

For our example here, let's assume you are stripping a chest of drawers. Remove the pulls from your chest of drawers and set them aside in a safe place. Also remove the drawers. Next, with plastic and paper down to protect your floor, pour about one inch of paint remover into a saucepan.

The application of the paint remover is important because paint remover that is allowed to drip on or run over finished areas will cause spots or runs in the wood, which are difficult to remove. Paint remover should always be applied with a brush from the bottom of a piece to the top, working *with* the grain. When hand-stripping a larger piece, like a chest of drawers, work in sections. This method gives a feeling of accomplishment (as opposed to tackling the whole project at once) and prevents the drying of the paint remover. Apply paint remover to one section and wait for a reaction to occur. Then apply a second coat. Work the brush into the finish

to see if a reaction is taking place. If the brush tends to grip the old finish, more paint remover is needed. If, however, the old finish spreads like stain under your brush, an effective reaction has occurred, and the section may be wiped off with a towel (wiping with the grain, of course). It will often help to dip the towel in the clean paint remover before wiping the section down. This will ensure that you have an evenly stripped surface.

Begin applying paint remover with the three-inch brush, from the bottom of the piece to the top, with the grain. The best way I've found to work with paint remover is to hold a saucepan in one hand and work with the brush in the other, keeping the saucepan close to your workpiece. This helps to ensure that a maximum amount of paint remover is applied, and you won't drip paint remover all over the floor in the process.

Paint remover is most effective at full strength. That is why I recommend you put only one inch of it in your saucepan. When the supply in your saucepan is running low, add another inch of paint remover. This will strip much more effectively than paint remover poured out in large increments, which will end up a muddy mess as you dip your brush covered with old finish in it again and again.

Ventilation and Disposal

It is important to say a few words about ventilation. If you could see the vapors coming from the paint remover in the saucepan, it would look like dry ice melting. These vapors flow over the edge of the saucepan and fall to the floor. Thus, you may want to elevate the piece you are stripping. The vapors from the paint remover will seem very mild at the beginning of the stripping process, and will become consistently stronger as you work. You probably won't notice the toxic smell as it gets stronger and stronger. Of course, this depends on the size of the room and where you are working. It is best to be sure the room is ventilated to prevent an accumulation of toxic vapors, no matter how large the room is. There is no reason for you to inhale toxic fumes unnecessarily.

Paint remover requires special considerations for disposal. I have learned that there are few guidelines for homeowners when it comes to disposal of toxic materials. It may be that you can call the local landfill for some advice, but don't expect too much help. Some areas do have a hazardous waste pickup, but if that's not an option, I recommend that you spread plenty of kitty litter on the old paint remover, bundle up the newspapers or whatever else you have used for a floor covering, put the whole mess in a plastic bag, and throw it away.

STRIPPING A CLEAR FINISH

Supplies

1 gallon of liquid paint remover

Old saucepan, with a handle

3-inch paint brush

2-inch paint brush with the bristles cut down to 1 inch

Supply of clean cloths (two old towels, cut in pieces, would suffice)

Covering to protect the floor if you are working inside. It is best to work either in your garage or outside.

Pair of rubber gloves

Well-ventilated work area

Clean scraper

The Process

Apply a generous amount of paint remover to one area of your workpiece. Make sure to control the movement of your paint brush, so as not to flick paint remover across the room. When you come to the end of a brushstroke, stop the brush completely, rather than allowing the bristles to flick upward. If you don't do this, you may need to refinish a couple other pieces of furniture.

Be patient and wait for a reaction to occur between the paint remover and the old finish. This is very important.

Apply a second full coat of paint remover to improve the reaction and aid in dissolving the old finish.

At this point one of three things will be required.

1. If the finish and the paint remover have reacted properly, the finish may be soft enough to simply wipe off with a piece of towel.

2. You may need to wipe off the old finish with a piece of the towel dipped in the paint remover.

3. It may be necessary to remove the bulk of the old finish using a clean scraper. Keep in mind that the scraper is only to have mild pressure on the wood to move the old finish off the piece. The scraper should be used with the grain of the wood.

Lightening the color of the wood can be accomplished using fine steel wool (0000), scrubbing with the grain, and finishing by wiping with a cloth dipped in paint remover, again wiping with the grain.

A detail step is to check the corners, the molding or carved areas, etc. Removal of the finish in these areas can be accomplished using the two-inch brush with the bristles cut back. Gently brush paint remover into these areas and work it in with the bristles of the brush to dissolve the old finish. Wiping with a clean cloth will help remove the dissolved finish, but I prefer to continually brush in clean paint remover, which will dissolve the old finish. Continued brushing with clean paint remover will ensure areas that cannot be wiped off with the cloth will dry clean, with no traces of the old finish left behind.

The final step is to wipe the piece down with a cloth dipped in paint remover to ensure uniformity of finish removal. This last step is key because any small areas that are missed in the stripping process can turn into light spots after they are sanded out.

ADDED DETAILS FOR DOING TOP AND DRAWERS
First, the top can be stripped in one of two positions. You can strip it either upright or on end. In either position, the paint remover should be applied from end to end, with the grain and across the width of the piece. Care should be taken to prevent drips or runs down the sides or front of the piece. (You might note that a good refinishing job would not have runs down the back either.) If you are concerned about

drips or runs over the edges, it is best to set the piece on end, remembering to work with the grain from bottom to top.

STRIPPING PAINT

Supplies

Paste-type paint remover

Liquid paint remover

2-inch scraper

Pocket knife with a pointed, sharp blade

3-inch paint brush

2-inch paint brush with the bristles cut down to 1 inch

Old saucepan

Covering for your floor (this job, too, is best done either in your garage or outside)

Rubber gloves

Supply of clean rags

Well-ventilated work area

The Process

The preparation for stripping a painted piece is similar to the preparation for stripping a clear finish, but there are a few added suggestions I would like to put in here. You're probably wondering why there are two types of paint remover listed under "Supplies." First, paste-type paint remover has paraffin wax added to it to make it heavy-bodied. The reason for this is simple. The heavier paste facilitates a better reaction, as it allows a thicker layer of paint remover to sit on the surface for a longer time. Remember that most painted finishes are heavier than clear finishes, so the reaction will be slower on the heavier painted finishes. If you're not willing to sit back and let the paint remover do its job, you will be toiling and scraping and frustrated, just as I was twenty years ago slaving over my old Hoosier cabinet. This is not to mention the damage that can be done by scrapers gouging the wood, as well as coarse steel wool and sandpaper and water, all of which result in damage similar to that done by the dreaded lye tank.

The Process

Apply a coat of paste-type paint remover to a section of the painted workpiece. If the paint has an oil base, it will buckle as the paint remover reacts with the paint. If the paint is latex based, the reaction will be a dissolving action as opposed to a buckling action. An adequate time to wait for this reaction to occur is two to five minutes.

If the reaction is better in some areas than in others, apply more paint remover to the areas where the reaction is slower. You can test the reaction by gently moving the old paint with a scraper.

This will also tell you if there are multiple coats of paint that will need to be stripped. If there are multiple coats of paint, don't try to strip them all at once. It may be necessary to gently scrape off layers that the paint remover has reacted with and then apply another coat of paint remover. Follow this process of applying paint remover and scraping until you are down to bare wood.

This process will remove approximately 90-95% of the paint. The remaining paint (in the corners and grooves, etc.) is often time-consuming detail work that you will be very glad you did when you set this finished piece in your living room. Apply paste-type paint remover and work with the pocket knife and/or the 2-inch brush with the bristles cut down. Paint on and around the carvings is probably a heavier accumulation of paint than that on the flat surfaces of the piece and will require more time to react with the paint remover. The best way to strip these areas is to brush paint remover into them with the short brush. Repetitious brushing into these areas will help to speed the reaction of the paint remover with the built-up paint. The pocket knife is extremely handy for picking out small areas with paint in them and for doing the edges around panels.

At this point, you will want to apply the liquid paint remover for the cleanup stage. Apply a full coat of liquid paint remover to the section you have been working on. The reaction should be very quick, and the paint remover should be brushed on and wiped off with a clean cloth. This will give the section a

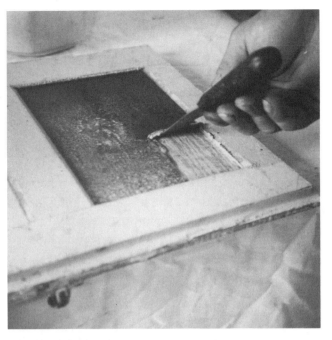

The paint remover is allowed to react with the paint and then removed with the scraper.

The paint in the grain is thicker; the brush helps encourage the paint remover's reaction with the paint down in the grain.

The owner tried to strip this door. What a mess!

I applied more paint remover, using steel wool and then a brush.

A pocket knife is used to gently remove paint from nicks and corners.

uniform appearance. If there are carvings, use cotton swabs to get the last of the paint remover out of these areas.

STRIPPING TURNED LEGS OR CARVED AREAS

Stripping the finish from turned or carved areas on a piece of furniture takes more time than working on a flat area, but it is not as troublesome as you might think. The finish on a carved or turned area may be heavier than on flat areas because the finish may have accumulated when it was originally applied. For this reason, it is important that you use enough paint remover and that the remover has time to react with the old finish. As with stripping any finish, patience and the reaction of the paint remover with the old finish are key to the process.

Supplies

Paint remover

3-inch brush

2-inch brush with bristles cut off to 1 inch

Gallon plastic milk jug with top cut off

Clean rags

Cotton swabs

The Process

Stripping the turned legs on a piece is much easier if you cut the top off a gallon milk jug, pour about an inch of paint remover into it, and set the foot of the leg in the jug. You can then brush paint remover on the leg, and it will run back down the leg into the jug. You may want to set each leg in a separate jug to speed up stripping all the legs. That way, you can apply paint remover to one leg and apply it to the

Place the carved or turned leg in the jug to contain the dripping paint remover.

Use the cut-off brush to work in the carved areas, brushing the old finish out.

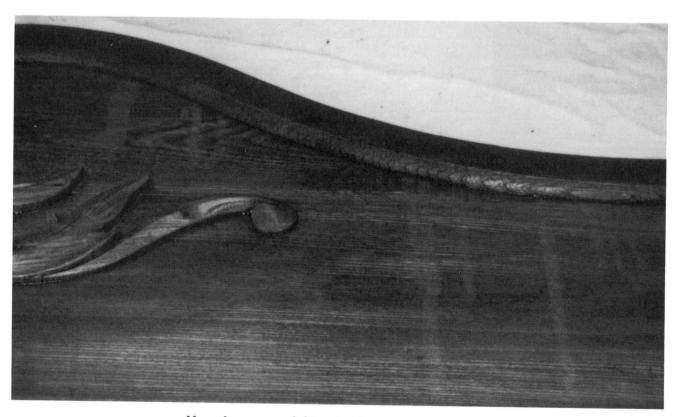

Note the runs and drips left by the paint remover.

These runs can be removed by wiping the piece down with clean paint remover and a clean cloth. Note the dirt on the cloth after the final wiping.

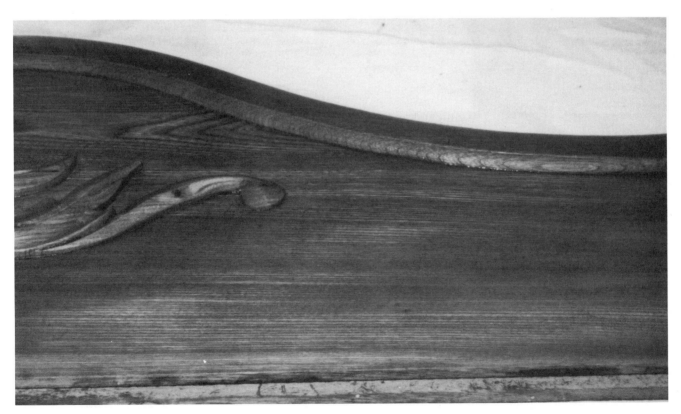

The finished piece.

others while you wait for the reaction to occur. Plenty of paint remover can be used for this without creating a huge mess. This method is also helpful for bedposts and other furniture with legs or posts.

Stripping carved areas is not the chore many believe it to be. It is helpful if the carved part can be laid down horizontally. In this manner, the paint remover can lie on the finish and not run off. Regardless, apply the paint remover and allow it to react with the old finish. Apply second and third coats of remover. As the paint remover reacts with the old finish, the paint brush with the bristles cut off will come in handy. Dip the cut-off brush into the paint remover and use it to brush *into* the old finish to enhance the reaction. Remove the old finish by brushing it away. When the finish is dissolved in the areas that are hard to get at, wipe the piece down with rags and finish up the small areas with cotton swabs.

SAVING THE PATINA

The patina is the look of aged wood. The look of the age in the wood is in the uppermost surface of the wood and can be destroyed easily. For this reason, it may be best to leave in some dents, gouges, and stains, as their removal would damage or destroy the patina.

Recently I inspected a walnut hunt table that dated back to 1820. It had been refinished and in the process, its patina had been completely destroyed. Whoever had done the refinishing had attempted to remove several stains from the top of the table by sanding. The stains were lightened, although still present in the table top, and this sanding had made the table top look different from the table legs and had greatly diminished the value of the table. In this case, the stains should have been left alone, thus retaining the patina and the value of the table.

I consider the patina a very valuable asset to a piece of furniture. Removing an ink spot could damage the patina and render a piece nearly worthless. It's best that some of the imperfections, which can add character, be left alone and the patina saved.

REPAIRS DONE BEFORE SANDING

The following repairs should be done before sanding a furniture piece:

- removing dents
- repairing cigarette burns
- repairing gouges to the wood
- removing stains in the wood

Removing Dents

Water is used to remove dents. Apply a small amount of water to the dent, until the level of the water is above the surrounding surface. It may be helpful to use a needle and press several holes into the center of the dent to enable it to absorb the water. Allow the water to penetrate for several minutes and then heat the area with the tip of an iron; do not allow the iron to touch the wood. It may be necessary to repeat this process several times to raise the dent.

Another method of raising dents is to place a cloth on the wood and dampen it over the dent. Then simply iron over the cloth. Be very careful when using this technique on veneered pieces, as the heat can lift the veneer. The previous method is preferable for veneered pieces because you can see the affected area clearly and watch for veneer failure.

Repairing Cigarette Burns

For a cigarette burn, the charred area will need to be scraped out with a knife to remove all of the blackened material. The depth of the burn will determine the repair needed. If the hole to be repaired can be lightly sanded, turning it into only a slight depression (like a dent), it can often be leveled with finish. Deeper holes will need to be filled with wood filler that matches the wood.

Repairing Gouges in the Wood

Gouges should first be lightly sanded and then filled with wood filler that matches the wood. Apply the wood filler with a putty knife. Fam-O-Wood is the wood filler I use, and it comes in different wood colors to match your piece of furniture.

Removing Stains in the Wood

I prefer removing stains in the wood with chemicals as opposed to sanding them out. The best chemical I have found to remove stain from wood is two-part wood bleach, available at most hardware stores. Simply mix equal parts of the wood bleach together and apply to the stained surface with a brush. Brush the bleach over the whole stained area, and use a hair dryer to help activate the bleach. You may need to repeat this process to remove the whole stain.

SANDING

Supplies

220 grit sandpaper

Sanding block

The Process

If the stripping has been done properly, in many cases the sanding step can almost be eliminated. Sanding with 220 grit sandpaper will help open the pores of the wood to accept stain. When sanding, your elbow tends to make an arcing motion, which can result in sanding *across* the grain. Be sure to sand *with* the grain of the wood. Also, when sanding care should be taken not to lighten edges or to oversand turned legs or carved areas.

Grit is the term used with sandpaper to identify the number of particles per square inch on the sandpaper. Therefore, the higher the number, the finer the sandpaper. Often, it will be necessary to sand out previous scratch marks caused by improper sanding using sandpaper that was too coarse. Coarser grits than 220 may be required if the piece has been refinished before and sanded improperly. However, I do not recommend using any sandpaper coarser than 120 grit. I also warn strongly against using belt sanders and orbital sanders, but if heavier sanding is required, use a vibrator-type sander, finishing with finer grits of sandpaper (220 or above).

STAINING

The types of stains you will most commonly find are:

- aniline dye stains
- non-grain-raising stains
- penetrating oil stains
- pigmented wiping stains

Aniline Dye Stains

The principal advantage of aniline dye stains, also called water stains, is that they can be readily mixed by dissolving aniline dye powder in hot water. After mixing a concentrated batch of stain, as described below, you can dilute the stain to any intensity you wish. You can even mix colors to make intermediate shades. These stains won't fade or bleed, and you don't need to apply a sealer coat before staining.

The disadvantage of these stains is that they will raise the grain of the wood. This can be remedied with a light sanding, however. Also, the aniline dye powders may not be available at your local hardware store, and you will need to take some time to mix and store the stains.

One last bit of advice: aniline dye stains do not penetrate well through old finish. It is most important when using these stains that the piece has been stripped carefully and thoroughly.

Mixing Aniline Dye Stains

Supplies

Non-aluminum pot

Distilled water

Aniline dye powder

Spoon

Glass bottle

The Process

After heating distilled water almost to the boiling point, add the aniline dye powder slowly, stirring constantly. Aluminum will alter the color of the stain, so you must use a cast-iron or glass container to heat the water. Add the dye in a proportion of 4 ounces of dye to a gallon of water. Stir to dissolve. After the powder is completely dissolved, let the stain cool before putting it in a glass bottle. This concentrated mixture can be modified by diluting it with distilled water or blending it with other aniline dye stains.

APPLYING ANILINE DYE STAINS

Supplies

Damp sponge

220 grit sandpaper

Sanding block

Concentrated aniline dye stain

Distilled water

3-inch paint brush

Scrub brush

Clean, dry cloth

The Process

First, raise the grain by wiping down the wood lightly with a damp sponge. After it has dried, sand it lightly with 220 grit sandpaper on a sanding block. Now the water stain will not raise the grain of the wood any further. The one area you must keep damp throughout this process is any open-ended area, such as the side of a table top. If you don't keep these areas wetted, they will absorb too much stain and stain darker than the rest of the piece.

Test the stain on the underside of the piece or on a piece of paper to see if you like the tint. Lighten as you like with the distilled water. Brush the stain on the wood with the 3-inch paint brush. Stain the end surfaces first, while they are still wet, and wipe the stain off immediately. Make long, smooth strokes to keep the stain as even as possible. After applying a full coat, shake the brush clean and go over the surface again to pick up excess stain until the surface has an even color. Use the scrub brush to get into any cracks or crevices you can't reach with the paint brush. After all brushing is finished and the surface is even, wipe it down with a dry cloth to pick up the last of the stain.

If there are areas that will not absorb stain to match the rest of the piece, you can open the pores by rubbing with fine steel wool while the area is still wet with stain.

Non-Grain-Raising Stains (NGR Stains)

Non-grain-raising stains start as powders, just as the aniline dye stains do, but they are dissolved in a solvent other than water. They don't bleed, and they dry rapidly. There is a wide variety of pre-mixed colors available, but you can also mix pigments as you wish, although the cost of the pre-mixed stain is roughly the same as the combined cost of the solvent and the powdered stain.

These stains dry so quickly that they are difficult to brush, and you are better off to spray them. A further difficulty with brushing is that the stain must be applied in such a wet coat that it may raise the grain anyway. When sprayed, it will never raise the grain.

APPLYING NON-GRAIN-RAISING STAINS

Supplies

Pre-mixed stain

3-inch paint brush

The Process

Brush on a heavy, wet coat of the stain with the paint brush. Work in sections. You could dilute the stain by half with mineral spirits and apply two coats of weaker stain to avoid overlapping brushmarks.

Penetrating Oil Stains

Penetrating oil stains, as their name suggests, penetrate into the pores of the wood, giving it a deep, rich color. They are easy to work with and are widely available. They work especially well on coarse-grained wood, which will often clog up with pigment if you use a wiping stain. The only hazard in using this type of stain is that it will penetrate deeply into a very porous surface and will be difficult to remove once it has penetrated. As long as you test the color of the stain before applying it, you should not have to worry about this.

Don't try to economize on the stain. A little bit goes a long way, and you will definitely see a difference if you use a lower-quality stain, because the colors are not very true.

Applying Penetrating Oil Stain

Supplies

Penetrating oil stain

Paint stirrer

2-inch sponge brush

Clean, dry cloth

The Process

After stirring the stain, apply a small amount with the sponge brush to the underside of the piece to check the color. Once you have the shade you want, brush on a thin, even coat with the sponge brush. Try to avoid overlapping. After giving the stain time to penetrate, wipe off the excess stain with the dry cloth. Allow the stain to dry twenty-four hours before applying the sanding sealer.

Pigmented Wiping Stains

Pigmented wiping stains consist of pigments suspended in a penetrating resin. This resin helps to seal the wood, which explains why these are also called *stain sealers*. They must be stirred continuously to guarantee that the pigment has not settled. This type of stain balances well, giving a uniform color, and one of the best uses for it is to stain a piece constructed from different woods. Pigmented wiping stains also work well on softwoods, such as white pine.

One thing you can do with pigmented wiping stains that you can't with any other type of stain is lighten the wood. White wiping stain is the best stain to use for this process.

Applying Pigmented Wiping Stain

Supplies

Pigmented wiping stain

Paint stirrer

2-inch sponge brush

Clean, dry cloth

The Process

Make sure the stain is thoroughly mixed. Brush it on with the sponge brush and allow it to penetrate the wood. Once the stain has begun to lose its sheen or has reached the desired tint, wipe it off with the cloth.

Pigmented wiping stains tend to darken wood very deeply, especially softwoods. If you wish to lighten the stain after it has been applied, dampen a second cloth with paint thinner and wipe carefully. This procedure can also be used to lighten spots that have stained too deeply.

Paste Wood Filler

Paste wood fillers are used to level the surface of wood, especially woods with coarse grains and large pores, such as oak, walnut, or chestnut. They are not always necessary, and generally closely grained woods will need no filler. Paste wood fillers can be purchased in colors to match the wood on which you are working, or in a natural shade with no pigment. Often they will need to be thinned before use. Naphtha or turpentine will thin filler easily. The appropriate viscosity for the filler is about that of thick cream. You must remember that the filler will be difficult to work with if it is too thick. At the same time, too thin a coat can damage the stain beneath.

Applying Paste Wood Filler

Applying paste wood filler requires correct timing and careful attention to detail. The key detail that can make this job much easier is having done all of the previous steps correctly. It is often best to seal the wood first with a *wash coat*. A wash coat is simply finish that has been thinned, generally nine parts thinner to one part finish. This has the effect of lightly sealing the wood pores.

Supplies

Stiff brush

2-inch paint brush, with the bristles cut down to 1 inch

Small squares of burlap

Clean cloths

The Process

Clean the surface of the piece with the stiff brush. Apply the filler quickly with the grain, dealing with one small section at a time. As you move to a new section, make sure to mix the filler thoroughly. Rub the filler into the grain slightly, then brush the surface smooth with the grain.

After the filler loses its sheen (about five to seven minutes), rub the filler into the wood across the grain and in a circular motion with a piece of burlap folded to about the size of your hand. This step requires correct timing if the filler is to be worked easily.

Take clean pieces of burlap and wipe off the surface, once again working across the grain. Continue this process, substituting cloths for the burlap, until all excess filler is removed and the surface is left clean and smooth. Once the surface has begun to shine, lightly wipe the surface down one final time, this time with the grain.

Once this process is complete, let the piece dry for at least twenty-four hours. A light sanding with 280 grit or 320 grit sandpaper should follow to remove any excess filler from the surface.

Sanding Sealer

Sanding sealer serves to prevent the stain in the wood from leaching through to discolor the finish. Varnish-based fast-drying sanding sealer is the best type to use for at-home refinishing projects. Make sure you have chosen a fast-drying sanding sealer, or you will end up wasting a day waiting for the sealer to dry.

Supplies

Varnish-based fast-drying sanding sealer

New 3-inch sponge brush

The Process

Using the new 3-inch sponge brush, brush a coat of the varnish-based quick-drying sanding sealer on the surface. Varnish-based sanding sealer will usually dry to the touch in ten to fifteen minutes, so working time is limited once it has been brushed on. Using a small amount of sealer on the brush at one time will help you avoid runs and drips, which is important because going back to fix a drip or run can just make matters worse. After two to three hours,

the sanding sealer should be completely dry and ready to sand. Test the hardness of the sealer by pressing your thumb down on the surface. If it leaves a print, it should be left to cure a while longer. (The thumbprint will just sand off in the next step.)

SANDING THE SEALER

Sanding sealer has similar ingredients to those found in soap. As you might surmise, it sands off very easily. This step should be done lightly and carefully to make sure you don't completely undo the previous step. Use 220 grit sandpaper on a sanding block, and let the weight of the sanding block do the work. Just slide the block back and forth over the sealer.

A word about using sandpaper as opposed to steel wool. Sandpaper on a sanding block will *level* the finish, whereas steel wool will *smooth* the finish. This is important, as the sandpaper will cut down raised areas or specks of foreign matter that may be in the finish. Steel wool leaves behind many small steel particles that can be difficult to remove and may show up in the coats of finish.

APPLYING THE FINISH

Supplies

Damp cloth

Benjamin Moore One-Hour Finish

3-inch sponge brush

Small quantity of water

600 grit wet/dry sandpaper

Sanding block

The Process

Benjamin Moore One-Hour Finish dries so quickly that it doesn't accumulate particles of dust like other, slower-drying finishes tend to. That's the main reason I recommend it. Before applying the finish, wipe the entire piece down with the damp cloth. Apply a coat of finish to one section of the piece at a time, using a 3-inch sponge brush. After you have brushed a first coat on the whole piece, wait until the finish is dry. Then all you will need to do is sand the finished surface. Use 600 grit wet/dry sandpaper on a sanding block. You can use the sandpaper without the sanding block for areas such as carvings that the block cannot reach, but be careful not to oversand. Use a small amount of water as you sand, then apply a second coat of finish.

French Finish

French finish (also called French polish) is a technique for applying shellac that goes back several centuries. It is impossible to achieve the appearance typical of a French finish by rubbing and buffing other finishes. Many thin layers of shellac need to be applied to build a French finish, and this can be a somewhat tedious process. The experience that French finishing reminds me of most is spit-shining my boots while I was in the Army. The first time I spit-shined my boots took much longer than reshining them when the first shine had dulled. Once the foundation has been laid down and the French finish achieved, it is easy to maintain with paste wax.

PREPARING THE SURFACE FOR A FRENCH FINISH

Supplies

400 grit sandpaper

Sanding block

Shellac

Denatured alcohol

2-inch sponge brush

Clean cloth

French finish can be applied over an older finish, but it must be cleaned first. This can be done with either DL Blue Label Hand Cleaner or by wiping the piece down with mineral spirits. French finishing can be done over a non-grain-filled finish but it will take much longer. A grain-filled finish looks even and smooth (like a piece of glass). Non-grain-filled finishes have very small lines where the finish has sunk into the grain. If you are new to French finishing, I suggest you work on a piece that is grain filled.

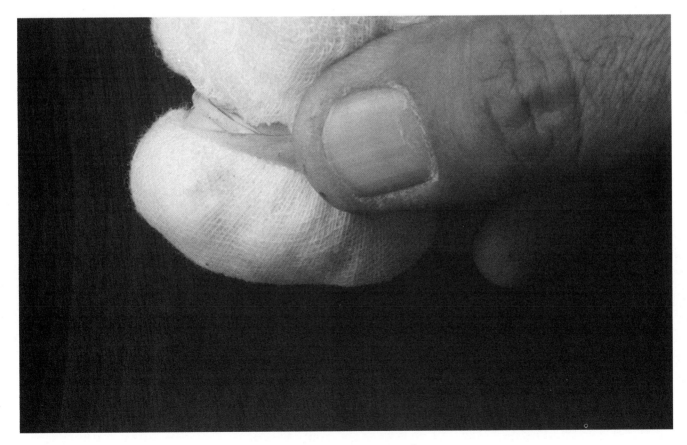

French polishing pad.

For new work or a piece you are refinishing, the grain can be filled in one of two ways: either by using a grain filler or by building enough finish that it becomes filled by the finish. I have described filling the grain with a filler earlier in this chapter. When applying a new finish that you wish to French finish, it is possible to fill the grain with several coats of shellac. The number of coats it will take depends on what type of wood you are working with. For example, if you plan to French finish a piece of oak, I suggest you forget the twenty coats of shellac you would need and simply use a grain filler. Cherry and maple take less time to build a grain-filled finish; mahogany and walnut more time. Oak, ash, and chestnut work best with a grain filler.

The process of filling the grain and preparing the surface for French finishing is simple. Apply a coat of shellac and sand it with 400 grit wet/dry sandpaper and water. Then apply the next coat. Remember to use a sanding block. This will cut the finish down but will not affect the finish that has sunk into the grain. When the finish in the grain has become slick and level like a piece of glass, you are ready to do the French finishing.

APPLYING THE FRENCH FINISH

I buy French finish pre-mixed so I don't have to fool with those pound cuts of shellac. Many furniture catalogs stock a French finish you can buy pre-mixed.

A few words of caution before you start rubbing:

1. The amount of material on the pad is very, very important. It is better to use too little than too much. Having the pad loaded with material can quickly ruin an hour's work. I've found this out the hard way many times, and it can be frustrating to say the least.

2. Do not allow the pad to stop on the work piece for even a second. Land the pad on the surface as if an airplane were landing and leave the surface in the same way. If you stop for a split second, you will see the damage done and how it will ruin all your work.

3. Table tops and the flat surfaces of your work piece will be easier to do. Other areas will require you to change the size of the pad or work with a loose piece of cloth or possibly a small sponge brush.

The Process

With pad in hand, load the pad with several drops of finish. The number of drops depends on the size of the pad you have made. Five to six drops is a good number to start with. Pat the pad into the palm of your other hand. This will disperse the liquid into the pad. Do this every time you add material to the pad. As I stated above, a concentration of liquid on the pad will damage your work. Land the pad on the surface and work in small circles. Move the pad in a rather quick motion, making small circles — about three to four inches in diameter. Go over the entire top of the piece being French finished to build the foundation. Moving the pad in a circular motion will cause light swirls, which will be removed later. Once the entire top has been padded over in small circles, begin to pad in larger circles. Then change to a figure eight pattern. As you increase the diameter of the circle, your pressure on the pad should become less and less.

With a good foundation laid, the light swirl marks can be removed in the following manner. Move the pad across the piece as if an airplane were landing and then taking off again. (These are called "touch and go" landings.) With very light pressure the swirls will begin to disappear until they are finally gone and your work is finished.

HOW TO APPLY FRENCH FINISH

Supplies

Lint-free cloth

Rubber band

Shellac

The Process

French finishing will prove an easier task if the layers of shellac are applied over a smooth, grain-filled surface (as described above). Shellac or lacquer is a good foundation for French finish. The process is begun by making a pad with which to apply the finish. Using an 8-inch square piece of soft, lint-free cloth, bundle the cloth to make a pad that has no creases at one end and place a rubber band around it to maintain its form.

Add drops of shellac to the pad to dampen it. (A small pad will take fewer drops than a large pad.) Tap the pad into the palm of your other hand to disperse the shellac into the pad. You want the pad touching the surface of the furniture piece to be damp, not wet.

There are two key items to remember about French finishing: (1) Don't apply too much material to the pad. (2) Never stop the pad on the piece you're working on. Either or both of these will cause damage to the finish.

With pad in hand, apply the finish to the surface of the workpiece like an airplane landing. Move in a circular fashion, without stopping. As you need to move off the piece to apply more shellac to the pad, move smoothly; don't pick the pad up off the piece. Keep building up the finish using a circular motion until the surface is covered. Start with small circles; when you have gone over the whole surface, make larger circles. Finally, switch to figure eights. Complete the process by swooping the pad across the piece from end to end, using the lightest pressure on the pad. Any circles or lines left from use of the pad will disappear with this motion.

When I learned how to French finish, I did not know how much it would aid me in my business. In my opinion, applying French finish is key to doing successful finish repairs. Learning this technique opened up a whole new phase for my business, as now I could go into customers' homes and repair damaged table tops or other damages to the finish. Damaged areas can be repaired with a burn-in. French finish is then applied over the burn-in, with color added to the finish. You would not be able to tell that a repair had been done.

USING SPRAY EQUIPMENT

While it is possible to describe how to use spray equipment, I must emphasize that the absolute best learning method is hands-on use.

There are four factors that must work together while spraying. They are:

- the material in the cup and how it is mixed;
- the air pressure at the gun;
- the pattern the gun is spraying; and
- the amount of material that the gun is putting out.

All four of these must be in harmony and functioning properly for a successful spraying job.

Material in the Cup

Thinning the material in the cup will help accomplish the following:

- Less air pressure will be required to push the material through the gun.
- Less *orange peel* will result as the material will flow out and level itself.
- The dry time window is lengthened by several seconds, thus allowing the material to flow out and "smooth" itself.
- Thinning helps prevent lap marks in table tops.
- Slowing the dry time will help prevent "blushing" caused by rapid drying and the material sucking in moisture. This causes the finish to turn a milky white.

As a rule, I usually do less thinning on the first coats as I want to build finish, and more on the final coats as this is when I am looking for a smooth finish applied over the finish I have built up.

Air Pressure at the Gun

Air pressure needs to be sufficient to push the material through the gun and onto the piece being sprayed. It must be enough to atomize the material properly but not so great as to cause overspray and push around the material already sprayed.

- Higher pressure will be needed to spray sanding sealer and heavy-bodied primers that will lose their properties if over-thinned.
- Moderate pressure is required for spraying final coats.
- Moderate to light pressure will help prevent overspray and orange peel on inside corners of cabinets and bookshelves.

The Pattern of Spray

The pattern of the compressed air spray is adjusted using the small screw knob at the top of the gun.

- Adjustment of the pattern will determine how the material is distributed over the piece being sprayed and the concentration of the material in any one area.

- A pattern that is too close will concentrate too much material in one area and cause runs unless extreme care is taken.

- A pattern that is too wide will fan out the material too far, wasting material if chairs are being sprayed or making it a slow process to lay a coat of material on a table top, thus creating lap marks because previously sprayed areas have begun to dry.

- To adjust the pattern, I turn the pattern screw all the way in and hold the gun in front of me, turned to its side so I can see the pattern. I begin to turn the pattern screw out to create a pattern that makes a 30 to 45 degree angle.

Material Adjustment at the Gun

Material put through the gun is adjusted by the second screw down on compressed air guns.

- Material should be sufficient to move the gun at a moderate pace, laying down enough material to coat the area but not so much that runs will occur.

- Material adjustment is made by turning the material screw in to minimize material and then back out.

- A test area is then sprayed, and the gun is adjusted to provide more or less material.

Putting It Together

With the gun loaded and connected to the air supply, spray a burst with the gun turned so you can see the pattern. Look for adequate material so the pattern can be clearly seen. If necessary, turn the pattern screw (top screw) all the way in and then adjust back out. Adjust the material screw (lower screw) all the way in and then back out. Turn the air pressure screw (below the handle) all the way in and then back out.

There are two other important aspects to mention here. The gun can be adjusted properly, but the application will depend on how the gun is handled. This includes how fast the gun is being moved and at what distance the gun is being held from the piece being sprayed.

Proper adjustment, distance, and movement must all be in sync. It takes hands-on practice to "get the feel."

SPRAYING LACQUER

Why Lacquer?

Years ago I received a call from a supplier who wanted to sell me lacquer to use in my business. I told him I did not use lacquer; varnish was my finish choice for pieces that needed to be refinished. He told me very matter of factly, "If you are not using lacquer, you don't know much about finishing," and hung up. Well, this guy really made me angry. I believed the finish I used did a good job. How dare he tell me I didn't know about finishing! It was shortly after I received that rather rude phone call that I decided to try out lacquer. Using lacquer is one of the things that helped me turn my shop into a professional furniture operation.

Lacquer cannot be used by the home refinisher because it must be sprayed on with professional equipment and facilities. However, it is important that you know about lacquer and understand how it is applied so you can better assess the state of your furniture and the type of finish it needs.

Why use lacquer?

1. Lacquer dries fast.

2. Lacquer can have toners (colors) added to enhance the appearance of the finish.

3. Lacquer can be repaired. A scratch on your table can most often be repaired in your home.

4. The bonding of lacquer is very different than oil or latex finishes. Each additional coat chemically bonds with the previous coat to form one coat.

5. Lacquer is durable and resists water and alcohol.

6. The sheen of a lacquer finish can be from dead flat to high gloss.

THE FINISHING PROCESS WITH LACQUER

1. The piece is put in the spray booth and sprayed with lacquer sanding sealer. Often the piece will be dry by the time I walk out of the booth.

2. We sand the piece using water from a spray bottle and 400 or 600 grade wet/dry sandpaper. Care is taken that edges and corners are not sanded through to the bare wood. The only purpose of sanding is to level the finish. Areas that feel smooth do not need to be sanded. So, with one hand we feel the finish and with the other we sand where necessary.

3. The piece is wiped down with a soft cloth to remove any water or dust. It is allowed to dry thoroughly and then placed in the spray booth again.

4. If adjustment to the color of the piece is required, a toner is added to the next coat of sanding sealer. Pieces can be toned to darken or enhance their color. A piece that has too much orange can be toned to a browner color by adding a green toner to the lacquer sanding sealer.

5. The piece is removed from the booth and sanded again with 600 wet/dry sandpaper and water. A sanding block is used on all flat surfaces to level the finish further.

6. Other color enhancements can be made by using a heavy-bodied glaze. This is applied by brush and wiped off with a soft cloth. If glazed, the piece if allowed to dry overnight before being sprayed again.

7. Depending on the piece, it may be sprayed as many as four times with sanding sealer.

8. The next step is to spray the piece with top coat lacquer. The sheen of the lacquer can be adjusted by adding a flattening compound, or the lacquer can be purchased in the sheen desired: flat, satin, or gloss. The number of top coats is up to the judgment of the person doing the spraying, but will most likely be at least three.

9. Each top coat is allowed to dry overnight to allow the lacquer to pack (cure).

10. Depending on the sheen desired, one of four things can be done to the top coat:

- It can be left as is.
- It can be rubbed with a cloth, oil, and pumice.
- It can be rubbed with steel wool and a compound.
- It can be sanded with wet/dry sandpaper.
- It can be buffed with a compound.
- A combination of the above.

Rubbing with a Cloth, Oil, and Pumice

Using a soft cloth, a rubbing oil is applied (vegetable oil works fine). A small amount of pumice and then sprinkled on and rubbed with the oil. This has the effect of reducing the sheen on a high gloss finish or adding sheen to pieces with a low gloss. The level of gloss depends on how much rubbing is done.

Rubbing with Steel Wool and Compound

For this process, 1/2 ounce of Murphy's Oil Soap is applied to a piece of super fine steel wool. The surface of the piece is misted with water from a spray bottle. The steel wool is then rubbed with the grain. Gentle pressure is required until the soap begins to foam at which time moderate pressure can be applied. This produces a flatter, hand-rubbed sheen.

Sanding the Finish

This is a good method for table tops. It is begun by sanding the top with 600 wet/dry sandpaper on a sanding block. The table top is lubricated by spraying a heavy mist of water mixed with several drops of dishwashing liquid. The water mixed with the drops of soap will perform two functions: it will lubricate the sanding, and it will keep the finish cooled and prevent it from melting due to the abrasion of sanding.

When the first sanding is complete, 1000 grit wet/dry sandpaper is used. (This must be obtained from an auto paint/supply store, as hardware stores do not usually carry it.) As with all wet sanding, several sheets of sandpaper are cut and put on the sanding block. As each sheet becomes worn, it is torn off and the next sheet used.

When the 1000 grit sanding is complete, 1200 grit wet/dry sandpaper is used, continuing to sand as described above.

With the 1200 grit sanding complete, the next step is to sand with 1500 grit sandpaper. By this time the finish is taking on a satiny sheen. As the scratch pattern is continually decreased, the sheen will appear.

When the 1500 grit sanding is done, the paper is changed to 2000 grit wet/dry sandpaper. Sanding with the 2000 will produce a beautiful satin sheen.

A special note to remember: steel wool will *smooth* the surface; sandpaper will *level* the surface. This is one of the major reasons I use wet/dry sandpaper instead of steel wool. The wet/dry sanding cuts down any particles standing up on the finish. Steel wool only smoothes them. The wet/dry sandpaper is cleaner and faster, and produces a level finish without the potential hassle of the steel wool particles.

Buffing the Finish

The professional way to finish a piece is with gloss lacquer, then to reduce the gloss by sanding or rubbing, and then to return the piece to the preferred sheen by sanding, rubbing, or buffing. Care must be taken when buffing a finish not to heat the finish to a point that it will cause harm. Particular care must be taken not to buff through to the wood at edges and corners. I use an automotive buffer that turns at a slow speed and also vibrates as it turns. I buff with a very fine buffing compound and then a clean, soft, dry cloth. This will produce a high gloss finish.

A GUIDE FOR YOUR FIRST REFINISHING PROJECT

1. Prepare a list of supplies you will need so your work will not be interrupted by an unnecessary trip to the hardware store.

2. Furniture with many parts such as a secretary desk, a roll-top desk, or kitchen cabinets will require disassembly to remove the old finish, then sand, stain, and finish. It will require patience and expertise to disassemble some pieces.

3. Painted finishes will often take three to four tries to strip. Make an effort to determine if the piece has a clear finish under the paint. This can be done by scraping off some of the old paint. Paint soaked into the wood grain will be difficult and frustrating to remove.

4. A clear finish on a chair will take about an hour to strip; a dining room table about one and a half hours; and a chest with three drawers about two hours. It may take longer if this is your first project or if there are carvings or turned parts to strip.

5. Uniformity is important. I have always felt that what you do to one area or section should be done to all. For example, sanding away a strip of finish on the top of a table that you missed while stripping will cause one area on the top of the table to be lighter and require sanding the whole top to that shade. Most likely the whole piece will have to be sanded. It would be easier to go back with paint remover to remove the old finish.

6. Stain charts in the hardware store are great for staining bare wood of the species shown on the chart, but are most often not very helpful when applying stain over a previously stained piece. If you are in doubt, purchase the smallest quantity and test on an inconspicuous area of the piece to be stained.

7. Wipe-on finishes require many applications to achieve the buildup and protection one coat of a brush-on finish will provide.

A tarnished brass escutcheon (keyhole cover).

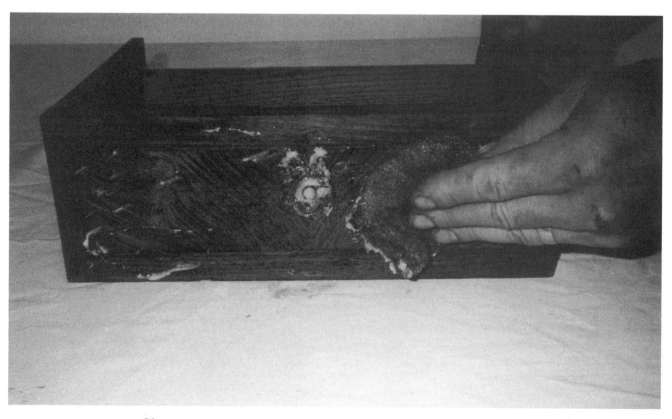

Cleaning the tarnish off with hand cleaner and fine steel wool.

Better than most brass cleaners, hand cleaner won't leave accumulations of dried white compound around the cleaned area.

SUMMARY: REFINISHING

- Stripping:

  The most important aspect of stripping is to use sufficient paint remover for a reaction to occur and give the remover enough time to react with the old finish.

  Do structural repairs before stripping.

  Work in a well-ventilated area.

  Apply paint remover with a brush from bottom to top of the piece with the grain.

  For painted pieces, use both paste-type paint remover and liquid remover.

- Save the patina!

- Use water and heat to remove dents as described on page 82.

- Cigarette burns can often be scraped out, sanded, and leveled with finish.

- Gouges should be lightly sanded, then filled with wood filler that matches the wood color.

- Stains in wood can be removed with two-part wood bleach, using a hair dryer to activate the bleaching process.

- Make sure you determine the type of stain you want to use, so as to utilize the correct technique for applying it.

- French finish:

  Clean the surface to be French finished with hand cleaner.

  Move the French finish pad smoothly, using a circular motion, across the piece.

  To finish the process, do stop-and-go "jet landings" with the pad to remove all marks.

- Using spray equipment:

  The material in the cup should be thinned.

  Make sure air pressure is sufficient to spray the material properly.

  Adjust the spray pattern so it is neither too wide nor too close.

7.
Kitchen Cabinets

How do the kitchen cabinets in your home look? If the cabinets in your kitchen need work, expect it to affect the value of your home. If you put your home on the market and sell it, the furniture you have will go with you to your new home, but your kitchen cabinets will stay in the old home.

Attractive kitchen cabinets will add to the beauty and value of your home. When my wife and I bought our home last year, the first room she went to was the kitchen. I always hoped when we drove up that she wouldn't want a house with kitchen cabinets that needed a lot of work. So if your cabinets do need work and you feel you would like to work on them, here are some ideas.

Making the decision as to what to do to your cabinets and then whether or not to tackle the job yourself may be of some concern. This is important, as you will be working in your kitchen. If your refinishing job is not well planned and organized, your kitchen could be a big mess for a long time. To make matters worse, if the desired result is not achieved and the job not done just right, you could take value away from your home.

The intent here is to suggest that you have a good plan for working in your kitchen. Know in advance the process you will use to achieve the desired result and get it done quickly so your kitchen can be put back in order.

Let's try to establish what will need to be done to improve the look of your kitchen cabinets.

1. Will cleaning or replacing the hardware add a new look to your cabinets that will be satisfactory?

2. Are you happy with the stain or color of your cabinets?

3. What is the condition of the finish? Has it become soft and discolored around the pulls?

4. Will your cabinets look their best painted?

First, let's look at what may be required to improve the looks of your cabinets. We'll start with the simplest ways to make your cabinets look better and go on to the more detailed.

HARDWARE

If the hinges and pulls are tarnished or dirty, it will detract from the beauty of your kitchen cabinets. Just cleaning and polishing the hardware will give a much improved look to the overall appearance of your cabinets. In ten minutes, you can brighten the looks of many of your cabinet hinges and pulls for just a few dollars.

Supplies

DL Blue Label Hand Cleaner

Superfine steel wool (00000)

Clean cloth for buffing

The Process

Cleaning tarnished brasses without removing them can often be accomplished by using DL Blue Label Hand Cleaner and super fine steel wool. Put some hand cleaner on the steel wool and rub the brass. Buff with a clean cloth. You will quickly see the improvement in the luster of the brass. Sealing the hardware with a brass sealer available at most hardware stores will prevent them from tarnishing for many years.

If the pulls are old and dated and the hinges tarnished, a big improvement will be to replace the pulls and replace or clean the hinges. Having the hardware clean and bright will improve the looks of most cabinets. As a word of caution, replacing hinges may turn into a nightmare, as the slightest difference in the hole pattern will change the position of the door and cause problems with it closing. It is best to remove the hardware from one door and purchase new hardware for it first, in order to test the new hardware and see if it will fit in the existing holes. This will give you an indication of what type of problems you may have installing the new hardware.

COLOR AND FINISH

Next on the list, you will want to look at the finish and color of the wood. There are several possible solutions if you aren't satisfied with the color of your cabinets.

1. Touch up the finish on your cabinets.
2. Revive the lifeless finish on your cabinets.
3. Refinish doors and drawers that have deteriorated or have a soft finish to match the original color.
4. Refinish the whole set of kitchen cabinets.
5. Paint the cabinets.
6. Replace one or two sets of doors with wood-framed glass doors.

If you are satisfied with the wood color and would like to repair the damaged, soft finish around door and drawer pulls, it can be done if the soft finish is in its early stages and hasn't discolored or caused damage to the stain. We do this frequently, and it is something you can do yourself if you wish to take the time.

REPAIRING A SOFT FINISH

Supplies

Varnish-based fast-drying sanding sealer
Polyurethane

DL Blue Label Hand Cleaner
220 grit sandpaper
3-inch sponge brush
Towel, cut into pieces

The Process

Remove the door with the soft finish. Use DL Blue Label Hand Cleaner on a piece of towel to clean the door. Lightly sand with 220 grit sandpaper, using care both when cleaning and sanding over the soft area. Apply a coat of varnish-based, fast-drying sanding sealer and allow it to dry. Test the soft area to be sure that it has dried and hardened. You can usually tell if it is not dry because it will have a wet sheen compared to the rest of the door. If the soft area has not dried completely, apply a second coat of varnish-based, fast-drying sanding sealer to that area only. It's important that you use a fast-drying sanding sealer, or the soft area may never dry. It may be necessary to repeat this a third time.

When all is dry on the door, lightly sand with 220 grit sandpaper, and apply a coat of polyurethane. This process will repair the damage to the soft area without requiring refinishing, but it may leave the sheen of the door somewhat different from that of the other cabinet doors in your kitchen.

It may be necessary to apply a coat of polyurethane to all the doors and trim. Often this can be done without removing the doors. It would be best to wipe the cabinets down with mineral spirits and lightly sand with 220 grit sandpaper before applying the finish. The process of repairing the damaged finish may be a little slow, but applying a new finish to your cabinets should go rather quickly (depending on the size of your cabinets, two to three hours).

REPAIRING A SOFT FINISH THAT IS BADLY DISCOLORED OR HAS GONE TO BARE WOOD

It's possible to refinish the cabinet doors and drawers that are in bad condition without having to refinish your whole set of kitchen cabinets. I have done this procedure hundreds of times to kitchen cabinets to restore them to their original condition. Often the cabinets will look better than when they were first installed, and this is especially true if new hardware is added. Regardless of whether you do it yourself or have someone do it for you, the savings in time and money are great.

Supplies

Liquid paint remover

Rubber gloves

220 grit sandpaper

Sanding block

2-inch scraper

Several 3-inch sponge brushes

Old saucepan to hold the paint remover

Mineral spirits (paint thinner)

600 grit wet/dry sandpaper

Some old rags

Minwax stain that matches the original color

Varnish-based fast-drying sanding sealer

Benjamin Moore One-Hour Finish or polyurethane

Reversible drill and screwdriver bit

Well-ventilated work area

Ladder

The Process

First, you need to remember that to match the original stain color, it will be best to retain as much of the color in the door as possible. This can be accomplished by removing the old finish as gently as possible. Also make sure you are working in a well-ventilated area when stripping to prevent an accumulation of toxic fumes. You should wear rubber gloves to protect your skin.

REMOVING THE FINISH

Remove the doors and drawers that need to be refinished, using the reversible drill and bit. I've found that for a better match, when two doors are paired, refinish both, even if one of them is in good condition. I usually work on either two or three doors at the same time when stripping. Lay the doors flat on an old table and apply an even coat of liquid paint remover. Be sure that the paint remover has enough time to react with the finish. This may require applying a second or even a third coat of paint remover.

Ideally, it is best to dissolve the finish from the door using the paint remover. It may, however, be necessary to use the scraper, but do this gently, working with the grain of the wood. When the majority of the old finish has been removed, dip a clean rag in paint remover and wipe down the door with the paint remover. It's very important that all of the old finish is removed by the paint remover and not by sanding.

Turn the door over and strip the other side, being careful not to let paint remover get on the newly stripped front side.

SANDING BEFORE STAINING

Lightly and evenly sand the doors, front and back. This should be a very light sanding that will help open the pores of the wood to accept stain. Often sanding the wood before staining it can be omitted if enough of the original color is retained in the door.

TESTING THE COLOR

Running a damp cloth over the door at this point will give you some idea of how the door will look with finish on it. What I usually like to do is stain one door and put sanding sealer on it to see how closely it matches the original color. Do this by holding the door up to the spot from which it was taken down.

STAINING

If staining is required, mix the stain thoroughly and apply a light, even coat with the grain of the wood using the paint brush. I like to use a 3-inch sponge brush to apply the stain because I have better control over it. The stain can be wiped off immediately for a lighter color, or allowed to stay on for several minutes for a darker shade. Care should be taken that the stain is not allowed to run over the edges of the door and discolor the other side. I generally use a small amount of stain on the brush so that I can control where the stain goes.

When staining the reverse side, always lean the door against something, because laying it down flat or on something will affect the drying of the stain and the color of the door. Allow the stain to dry overnight.

APPLYING THE SANDING SEALER

Using a new 3-inch sponge brush, apply a coat of the varnish-based sanding sealer to one side of each door, one door at a time. Set each aside and let them dry. Varnish-based sanding sealer will usually dry to the touch in ten to fifteen minutes. Because it dries so quickly, the working time is limited once it has been brushed on. Be very careful when going back to repair a run or flaw, as you could make the situation worse. Using a small amount of sealer on the brush at one time will help you avoid runs and drips. The doors should be ready to turn over and have sealer applied to the reverse side in about two to three hours.

You can test the hardness of the sealer by pressing your thumb down on the surface. If it leaves a print, it should be left to cure a while longer. (The thumbprint will just sand off in the next step.)

SANDING THE SEALER

Lightly sand each door with 220 grit sandpaper. As much as possible, I like to use a sanding block. This will help make a perfectly flat finish and makes it less likely that areas will be sanded through, which might mean having to restrip that door and start all over. Sand each door front and back.

APPLYING THE FINISH

I like to use Benjamin Moore One-Hour Finish because it dries so quickly that it doesn't accumulate particles of dust as slower-drying finishes tend to do. Before applying finish, it's best to wipe each door down with a damp cloth. Apply a coat of finish to each door, using a 3-inch sponge brush. When dry, apply a coat of finish to the reverse side. After this is dry, all you will need to do is sand the finished surface with 600 grit wet/dry sandpaper, preferably on a sanding block. Use a small amount of water as you sand. Apply a second coat of finish.

Now the doors should be complete. Before rehanging the doors, it's best to clean the base portion of the cabinets with mineral spirits and lightly sand with 220 grit sandpaper. Apply a new coat of finish to the base and other doors that did not need refinishing for a uniform sheen. It might be a good idea to take the doors down to apply the new coat of finish. It should take only one coat of finish.

REFINISHING A SET OF KITCHEN CABINETS

If you are not happy with the color of your cabinets, or if they are painted and you want to remove the paint, it will be necessary to strip the entire set of cabinets to bare wood and apply a new stain and finish. Again, if you wish to tackle this you can certainly do it with some time and patience. This job will be easier if you write out a list of materials and tools you need and have a definite plan to get the job done. You will be working in your kitchen, and you won't want to make a mess of your kitchen for months with a project that is dragging on forever.

Supplies

Paste-type paint remover

Liquid paint remover

220 grit sandpaper

Sanding block

2-inch scraper

Several 3-inch sponge brushes

3-inch paint brush

Two old saucepans to hold paint remover

600 grit wet/dry sandpaper

Rags

Stain of the desired color

Varnish-based fast-drying sanding sealer

Benjamin Moore One Hour Finish or polyurethane

Fan to ventilate the kitchen

Reversible drill and screwdriver bit

Masking tape

Plastic gallon jug with the top cut off

Spray bottle filled with water

1 pint mineral spirits (paint thinner)

Stepladder

The Process

REMOVING THE CABINET DOORS

Use the reversible drill and bit to remove the cabinet doors and drawers. It is a good idea to number each cabinet door by scratching a number into the wood behind the hinge plate. This mark will be covered when the hinges are placed back on the door. I suggest you do the stripping work in your kitchen first and get that out of the way.

STRIPPING THE FRAME

It doesn't matter what you strip first, but I recommend that you strip the frame in your kitchen first and get it done. That way, your kitchen is not completely out of commission while you're out in the garage stripping and finishing the cabinet doors. You want to begin by using the paste-type paint remover, because it will cling better to a vertical surface than liquid paint remover will. But before you start using paint remover in your home, find a window in which you can place the fan to blow out. It will vent the toxic fumes given off by the stripper. You should also put some type of covering on the floor and your counters. It may be necessary to tape off some areas that butt up against the wall or the ceiling.

Begin by pouring one to two inches of paste-type paint remover into a saucepan. It's best to continually add new paint remover to the saucepan rather than pouring in a whole bunch that you may not use. In addition, this will keep the paint remover at full strength. Start at the bottom and work up, as you apply the paint remover. Work in one section at a time or, for a heavier finish, you may work in two sections at a time. A section is an end panel or one block of trim (where two doors would fit). Apply the paint remover to the second section and go back to the first section, giving the paint remover time to react with the finish on the second section.

When the first section is finished, go to the third section and apply a coat of paint remover, then strip the second section. This is simply a way of allowing the paint remover enough time to react with the finish without your having to sit and wait for the reaction. It will most likely be necessary to lightly scrape the old finish off with the scraper. Immediately after scraping a section, while wearing rubber gloves, dip a rag in the liquid paint remover and wipe down the section you just scraped.

It is important that you test to see if the paint remover has had enough time to react with and dissolve the old finish. You can easily tell if it has had a good reaction by test scraping an area or by brushing into the finish on light finishes to see if the old finish has broken down. Most clear cabinet finishes are not that heavy and should dissolve easily with an adequate amount of paint remover. The reaction of the paint remover with the old finish is extremely important. It will make the old finish much easier to remove and will make each of the subsequent steps much easier.

IMPORTANT STRIPPING HINTS

- Have the room ventilated.
- Start at the bottom and work up with the grain when applying the paint remover.
- Work in sections.
- Test to make sure the paint remover has reacted with the old finish for easy removal.
- When you begin stripping a section, finish it.
- *Do not* use water to remove the paint remover.

SANDING BEFORE STAINING

Sanding your cabinets will be a very easy chore, *if* (a very important "if") you have taken the time while stripping your cabinets to make sure that all of the old finish is removed — the hard part is over. Now you can do some very quick sanding with the 220 grit sandpaper on a sanding block. Depending on the size of your cabinets, it should take no longer than an hour or two to sand your whole cabinet frame. If you have done the stripping right, you could almost eliminate the sanding step, because although the liquid in the paint remover does tend to raise the grain slightly, the wood should still feel smooth. Light sanding will help open the pores of the wood for better stain penetration.

IMPORTANT SANDING HINTS

- Don't use any sandpaper coarser than 220 grit.

- Cut the paper in strips and put several sheets on the sanding block at once.

- Tear off the used piece of sandpaper from the sanding block and go to a fresh sheet rather than trying to get too much out of one sheet of sandpaper.

- Do not sand out remaining old finish that you may find as you sand the piece. Remove it with liquid paint remover.

STAINING

Before staining, it is wise to vacuum up any dust that may have accumulated from the sanding process. Wipe the cabinets down with a damp cloth. There are several types of stain that you could use, and it may be easier to work on vertical surfaces with a heavier-bodied stain. You may want to take one of the smaller doors to a hardware store and have the salesperson help you with testing stain on the back of one of the doors.

Once you have chosen the appropriate stain, staining is a simple process. I like to use sponge brushes when applying stain because I can better control the application of the stain than with a bristle brush. Also, you will not have nearly the problems with drips off the brush using a sponge brush that you would with a bristle brush.

Do your stain work very much as you did your stripping, working in sections. It may be that you can stain one section and immediately wipe it. If you want a darker color, stain two sections and go back to wipe the first. Then stain the third section and go back to wipe the second section, etc.

Apply the stain from the bottom up, working with the grain. You should avoid runs and drips on bare wood. The best way to do this is not to load up the brush with stain. Put small amounts of stain on the brush, and it will be easier to control. Use a soft cloth, working with the grain, to wipe off the newly stained areas. Like the sanding, staining will go quickly if you have done the previous steps properly. As you can see, each step in the refinishing

process is important to the next. Again, the first and most important step is doing the stripping right.

IMPORTANT STAINING TIPS

- Don't depend on stain charts for the color.

- Test colors on the inside of a cabinet door.

- Use a sponge brush to apply the stain evenly; avoid loading up the brush with too much stain.

- Darker tones can be achieved by allowing the stain to penetrate longer.

- Allow the stain to dry overnight before putting on the sanding sealer.

SANDING SEALER

Sealing does just what the word says. It seals the wood and helps protect it. This is important in your kitchen because the better your cabinets are sealed, the more protected they will be from the harmful effects of heat, humidity, grease, and water. Also, the sanding sealer sands very easily, makes for a very smooth finish, and dries quickly. Again, I like to use a sponge brush to apply the sanding sealer for the same reasons I like to use it to apply the stain. One coat of varnish-based sanding sealer is usually enough. By the time you're finished brushing the sanding sealer on the cabinets, most of them will be dry. Once the cabinets are dry, they are ready to be sanded.

Lightly spray the area to be sanded with water from the spray bottle. Using the sanding block with 600 grit wet/dry sandpaper on it, sand the area. One or two strokes should smooth the area, and you can tell when it's smooth enough by running your hand over it. Change the sandpaper as it fills with the sealer. You will see dots on the sandpaper as it fills with sealer. If you don't change the sandpaper frequently enough, the dots will get larger and rub streaks in the finish. This whole job should take no more than three or four sheets of sandpaper, with each sheet cut into four pieces. When you finish sanding an area, wipe it down with a dry cloth.

IMPORTANT SANDING SEALER TIPS

- Sanding sealer dries fast, so you have a limited working time.

- Don't overload the sponge brush with sanding sealer.
- Sand only until the surface is smooth; avoid excessive sanding.
- Change the piece of sandpaper you're working with often to avoid marring the finish.

THE FINISH COATS

It is best to thin the finish coat by one-fifth with paint thinner. That is to say, mix four parts polyurethane with one part paint thinner. This will help the polyurethane to flow out and even itself better. Applying the finish coat is a simple process. Just brush on the finish coat with a sponge brush and look for runs as you go along. Allow the first coat to dry, and see how it looks and feels. If it feels a little rough, do a light sanding with 600 grit wet/dry sandpaper and water to the rough areas. Apply a second coat of finish. It is best to wait overnight before applying the second coat of finish, if needed.

Now that the frame and trim are refinished, all that is left are the doors and drawers. Simply refer to the section earlier in this chapter for directions on refinishing cabinet doors.

PICKLING CABINETS

A pickled finish on your cabinets takes more time and patience than other types of finishes, but it can add a great deal of beauty and value to your home. So what is pickling and how do you do it? I think of a pickled look as one that is not a wood stain color; rather it is a paint stain color. Many people may think of pickled finishes as being white. Colors such as brown, tan, orange, red, etc., are all familiar wood stain colors. But what about white, blue, or green? Almost any color that is not what you would think of as a natural wood color can be a "pickled" color. Can you do a pickled finish yourself? You can. It will take some extra time, but the results will be well worth your efforts.

The first time I pickled a set of kitchen cabinets was six years ago. It was a very enjoyable job because I was working for an interior designer who knew exactly how she wanted her cabinets to look. It is a satisfying challenge to work for someone who knows what he or she wants, especially when it comes to a custom stain, a special finish, or both.

This job was a challenge because we had to match the new island built in the kitchen to the rest of the cabinets. The cabinets were stripped, sanded, and stained with a white stain. They were then sealed with a varnish-based finish. The final touch was to add some additional white around the panels on the doors and to the crown moulding. I used a 1/2-inch artist's brush to add the final touches of white. I remember that I felt like Michelangelo as I added the final touches of white to the crown moulding around the ceiling. A dab of white here or a light streak of white there, and then a light wiping with a soft cloth. I left that job proud of my efforts, and the customer has since referred many furniture and cabinet jobs.

Pickling is similar to the process used to refinish cabinets. The difference is that all or most of the stain color must be removed. Therefore, cabinets with a dark stain on them will be more of a challenge than those with a lighter stain color.

Supplies

In addition to the supplies needed for refinishing your cabinets, you will need the following:

Two-part wood bleach

Hair dryer

Several 3-inch sponge brushes

White stain

Rubber gloves

The Process

Every set of cabinets I pickled has presented a unique challenge. Because of the variety of woods and stain colors, changing the color to a pickled look requires experimenting to obtain the look you want. Open-grain woods (oak, pine) will more easily achieve a contrast in color than close-grain woods (maple, cherry). Strip the cabinets as described in the section on refinishing. As it will be necessary to lighten the color of the wood, additional sanding may be required. This can best be accomplished by first sanding the cabinets with 120 grit sandpaper and then with a finer 220 grit sandpaper. You may also need to bleach the wood to the desired lighter shade. I suggest that you pick one of the doors and do some work to the back of the door as an experiment.

BLEACHING

Use two parts wood bleach applied with a three-inch sponge brush. The wood bleach will not work over areas that have finish remaining. Sanding will help open the pores of the wood to accept the bleach. Apply an even application of wood bleach in the same way you would apply stain. Work in sections and dry the bleach with the hair dryer. The hair dryer will aid in the reaction of the bleach with the wood. It may be necessary to re-bleach to obtain the desired lightness of the wood.

STAINING FOR A PICKLED LOOK

The whitewash pickled look may be achieved by several methods. One method may work better than another and again is an opportunity to experiment.

1. Your local hardware store has stains you can purchase that may do the job. It may be that a heavy-bodied stain will work better than a light-bodied stain.

2. White oil-base paint can be brush on then wiped off. The paint may be thinned with mineral spirits (paint thinner), then brushed on and wiped off.

3. White latex paint can be brushed on and wiped off. It can be thinned with water, brushed on, and then wiped off.

4. Any of the above materials may be wiped on to achieve the desired effect.

APPLYING SANDING SEALER

The color of many oil-base sanding sealers and top coats is amber. This can cause your cabinets to take on an almond tone. Have the salesperson at the hardware store open the can of sanding sealer and top coat finish to ensure the one you buy is clear.

For additional color, white enamel paint can be added to the sanding sealer. This would be for an oil-base finish. If you decide on a water-base finish, white latex paint can be added. When adding white to either oil or latex, start with a small amount (1/2 ounce to one quart). Too much can ruin your sealer by making it too white.

Apply one coat of sanding sealer and allow it to dry. Wet sand with 600 wet/dry sandpaper and use a spray bottle to mist the area to be sanding with water. Care should be taken not to sand too hard and rub through the finish.

Two applications of sanding sealer should be sufficient. If you have added color to the first coat, it may not be necessary to add color to the second. This is a judgment call by the refinisher.

While two coats of sanding sealer may be applied in one day, it is best to apply the top coat finish in one coat one day and the second the next day. Lightly sand between the two coats to ensure a smooth finish and proper bonding of the coats to the finish. While some people like to use steel wool between coats, I find it is a problem with all the steel wool particles. I do not have that problem with the wet/dry sandpaper.

Allow the finish to dry at least one day before you re-hang the doors. The handling required to hang the doors can easily damage a soft finish.

PAINTING CABINETS

Another option, last but not least, is painting your cabinets. Quite frankly, I have looked at many cabinets that would look their best painted. Lower-grade woods such as birch and western cedar are prime examples. Some commercially made cabinets are simply cheap cabinets. Once the paint is on them, only you and the manufacturer will know what they are really made of. You may be surprised at how great your cabinets look painted and how clean and neat your kitchen will look.

Supplies

220 grit sandpaper

Sanding block

Mineral spirits

Stain-killer primer

Latex enamel paint (you choose the color and sheen)

4-inch roller

8-inch roller and roller pan

3-inch or 4-inch trim paint brush

Covering for the floor

Masking tape

Stepladder

Rags

The Process

PREPARATION FOR PAINTING

Preparing your cabinets is important, very important. In most cases, it will not be necessary to strip them, but it is crucial that they be cleaned thoroughly. This can be done with mineral spirits (paint thinner). Cleaning the cabinets will have the effect of removing any grease or grime and any finish that has become soft. However, if the finish has deteriorated badly, it may be necessary to strip some areas with paint remover.

Now is the time to fill any holes in the surface. Simply use spackling compound, applied with a small putty knife or your finger. The spackling compound will sand easily and is the simplest way to fill holes from old hinges, if you are going to replace them.

The next step is to sand. You do not need to sand your cabinets down to bare wood but rather to scuff sand, creating a scratch pattern to give the paint a good bond. As you sand, the sandpaper will find spots for you that need additional cleaning, as the sandpaper will load up quickly when it hits a soft or greasy area.

To prime your cabinets, I strongly recommend you use a shellac-based stain killer primer. This is a good primer that will prevent any stain from bleeding through the paint. My sister-in-law painted her cabinets and didn't use a primer, and many areas changed color from stains bleeding through.

Prime the cabinets and allow the primer to dry. Check to ensure that no stains are bleeding through the primer. Apply a second coat (and possibly a third coat) of primer to any heavily stained areas.

PAINTING

As a top coat, I use a good latex enamel paint. You can roll both the primer and top coat, and the 4" roller is excellent for painting hard to reach areas inside your cabinets. After rolling, follow with a brush for a smooth finish. The most time-consuming step is painting the insides of your cabinets (if you decide to do this) and painting the doors.

Best results will be obtained by removing the doors and drawers to do the painting. Using a reversible drill with a screwdriver bit to remove the doors will make the job go much faster. Years ago I took down cabinet doors and put them back up with just a screwdriver. It always took a long time and I wouldn't consider going back to the old way.

Cut the top off a one-gallon plastic milk jug to keep all the hardware in as you take the doors down. It is wise to number the doors by scratching a number behind the hinge plate, which will be hidden when the door is re-installed.

We use a rack to hold the doors as they are being painted or refinished, and you may be able to improvise the same by purchasing 1" x 1" x 8' fir strips from the building supply store and constructing a simple rack. They only cost about fifty cents each and are a big help. Care should be taken when turning the doors over to paint the backs, as the paint may feel dry but will take about ten to fourteen days to cure. You should cut strips of wax paper to cover the fir strips to prevent the paint on the doors from sticking to the strips.

The final touch is to clean or replace the hardware, as described earlier in this chapter. If you plan to replace hinges, be prepared for some problems. Try a set on a door before you start. It is best to try out the new hinges before you get to the end of your work and find out the doors won't close.

SUMMARY: KITCHEN CABINETS

- Clean dingy hardware in minutes with hand cleaner and steel wool.
- Replace hinges and pulls that are heavily tarnished or out of style.
- To repair a soft finish:

  Clean with hand cleaner.

  Sand lightly.

  Apply sanding sealer.

  Sand again and apply polyurethane.
- To repair a badly discolored finish:

  Strip off the old finish.

  Sand.

  Test the color.

  Stain.

  Apply sanding sealer.

  Sand.

  Apply finish, sand, and apply a second coat of finish.
- To refinish a set of kitchen cabinets:

  Remove doors and drawers, numbering as you go.

  Strip the frame, then doors and drawers.

  Sand.

  Stain.

  Apply sanding sealer.

  Finish with polyurethane.
- To achieve a pickled finish:

  Sand.

  Bleach with two-part wood bleach and dry the bleach with a hair dryer.

  Use the technique you have chosen (as described on page 102) to get the pickled finish.

  Apply sanding sealer, sand, and apply finish coat.
- To paint cabinets:

  Clean cabinet surfaces thoroughly.

  Fill holes with spackling compound.

  Sand for better adhesion.

  Prime with stain-killer primer.

  Paint with latex enamel.

Part III

Wood Used in Furniture

8.
Veneer and Inlays

Veneer has an undeserved bad reputation, dating from the nineteenth century when it was used to cover up shoddy workmanship on mass-produced furniture. One hundred fifty years prior to this, veneered furniture had only been available to the wealthy. As companies like the Dutch East India Company and its British competitors pioneered new routes to the tropics, exotic veneer woods became more accessible and popular.

Veneer and inlays are two excellent ways to give a wood without much figure to its grain, such as pine, a lot of character. Veneer can turn an indifferent-looking piece into a thing of beauty. Inlays add to the beauty of a piece in much the same way as veneers do. They have the added advantage of interrupting the pattern in the piece of wood in which an inlay has been placed and introducing an entirely new decorative motif.

People have been veneering furniture for thousands of years, dating back to ancient Egypt. The materials have changed, but the intent has always been the same: to cover a less valuable or less attractive material with a thin layer of beautiful, often costly material. Early civilizations used such materials as mother-of-pearl, ivory, tortoiseshell, and precious stones and metals. Today veneering is done mainly with wood, generally exotic woods so expensive as to make it prohibitively costly to produce whole pieces from them.

ADVANTAGES OF VENEER

In addition to cost considerations, there are three other advantages to veneer. Many of the woods that produce attractive veneer have no structural strength, and burls (dome-shaped growths on trees) from any type of tree would warp if used for solid construction. By slicing these woods into veneer, we can emphasize the positive points of the wood, especially its beauty, and ignore the negative aspects, such as structural weakness. Furthermore, woods that are burled or mottled are very scarce, and slicing them into veneer makes it possible to enjoy their beauty on many pieces of furniture.

Another aesthetic benefit of veneer is that inlays, marquetry, and many other patterns can be laid out with veneer that would be impossible to create with solid lumber.

STYLES OF VENEER

Just as the furniture styles described elsewhere in this book had preferred designs and decorative motifs, so many of them also had preferred veneers. In the Jacobean period (1660-80), oak was the prevalent wood for construction, but walnut was the preferred wood for veneering, a position it held until the rise of Thomas Chippendale and his school. In the William and Mary era (1688-1715), the designers applied the wood as marquetry, a style of veneering in which pictures, often in a floral motif, were constructed from different colors and shapes of veneer.

Circumstances changed in the middle of the eighteenth century, making mahogany more widely available than ever before. Chippendale arrived on the scene at the same time. He veneered almost exclusively with mahogany, but while mahogany is still a favored veneer wood, the designers who came after Chippendale did not admire it as he did. George Hepplewhite used fine crotch mahogany, but he preferred to work with the exotic "Amboyna Burl." Sheraton clearly preferred satinwood over any other veneer.

The veneering preferences of the nineteenth century are not too relevant, considering that the goal of using veneer for the mass-produced furniture of that period was not to beautify the wood, but merely to cover up ugly handiwork.

CUTTING VENEER

To fully appreciate the beauty and value of veneer, you must first understand the process that gives us sheets of wood $1/32$ inch thick from hundred-foot tall trees whose trunks you couldn't put your arms around. The felling of the tree, while a tough job, is the easy part of this process. The felled tree is taken out of the jungle, where many of the most exotic veneer woods grow, in various ways. In Burma, elephants drag logs out of the jungle, and in other locales, tractors, ox teams, and even people pull logs to rivers, on which the logs float to the seacoast. The logs are stored in water while they await processing. After preparation by spending several hours (or several days, depending on the hardness of the wood) in very hot water, the logs can be cut.

Slicing

Veneer can be cut in several different ways. The easiest and most common is slicing, which produces "half-sawn" veneer. The logs are cut in half on a vertical axis and are then placed on a long carriage. This carriage feeds the half log to a blade as much as 15 feet long, which cuts it across the grain into slices about $1/28$ inch thick. If you have ever seen ham sliced at a delicatessen, you know exactly how the mechanism for slicing veneer works. (And you also are probably wondering why the deli can't get the ham any thinner than that.)

If a log will not fit in the carriage, it is sawed into slices about $1/20$ inch thick. This is not very efficient

when you consider that for each useable slice of veneer, there is a piece the same size as the notch made by the saw that is turned into dust. These logs are not cut by hand. Instead, they are fed into a large circular saw or bandsaw.

Quarter-Sawing

The second most common method of cutting veneer is to quarter-saw it. The log is cut in half twice, yielding four pie-shaped quarters. These are then cut on the carriage from the outside edge through to the heartwood.

Half-Round Slicing

Rotary slicing is the method used to produce plywood. The reason that this is of interest to us is that it will make it much easier to explain the process of half-round veneer slicing. In rotary slicing, a length of the log is mounted centrally on a lathe. An extremely sharp blade is placed on the edge of the log, and as the log spins on the lathe, the blade slices thin, extremely wide pieces of veneer. The blade is mounted in such a way that it can move in closer to the log as the log becomes successively narrower. It works just like unrolling a roll of paper towels.

As you might expect, half-round veneer slicing uses the same mechanism as rotary slicing. In this process, the half log is mounted tangentially on the lathe. With each revolution of the lathe, progressively wider slices of veneer are cut.

WHERE VENEERS ARE FOUND

Many different parts of a tree can produce veneer, and a few of these parts produce different figures in their veneer. The three main highly figured veneers are those from the stump of the tree, from a crotch of the tree where a branch and the trunk meet, and from a burl on the side of the tree trunk. Wood from burls and stumps tends to yield veneer with rather random figures. Burl veneer, in fact, often has holes and other imperfections resulting from the growth pattern of the tree. On the other hand, veneer cut from the crotches of the tree has a consistent "V" shape, making it perfect for matching.

Matching

Matching is one way to accentuate the beauty of the veneer. The patterns that occur naturally in veneer, while interesting and beautiful, can clash if not arranged properly. By matching the veneer, the craftsman can guarantee that the pattern of the veneer presents the most attractive facade possible.

There are several standard ways to match veneer. The simplest is the oxymoronic random matching, which can be matched however the craftsman sees fit. Book matching is done with all types of veneer. As the name suggests, this style involves the veneer being alternated in such a way that the back of the first strip of veneer meets the front of the second strip, giving a look much like the pages in an open book.

A third type of matching used with all types of veneer is slip matching. Strips of veneer are placed side by side, repeating the figure of the veneer. This technique is often used with quarter-sawn veneer, but any type of veneer can be effectively slip matched. Veneer matching can be done on a vertical orientation, but veneer panels are generally matched on a horizontal axis.

There are other methods of veneer matching, but these are not usable with all types of veneer. Diamond patterns, herringbone patterns, and "V"-shaped patterns work best with crotch, stump, and burl veneers, many of which would be useless for panels without manipulation due to their odd grains and figures. These types of veneer can also be used in elaborate four-way and butt matches.

INLAYS

Inlays are patterns made with small pieces of veneer set into (or inlaid into) the veneer or solid wood surface of a piece of furniture. As I mentioned earlier, many different substances have been used to make inlays, but the most common material is veneer. Inlays have some of the same advantages that veneer does. They provide a way to make woods that are very costly more accessible, both by making it less expensive to use them and by using less of the wood on a single furniture piece. They also have an appearance that could not be duplicated in solid wood or uncut veneer.

Inlays are often used in regular geometric patterns, perhaps outlining the top of a table or chest. Providing a clear contrast with the wave-like figures in the veneer it surrounds, inlays generally have an understated pattern, such as alternating chips of holly (a very white inlay wood) and ebony. Woods with subtle or no figure are often preferred for inlays so that attention is not taken away from the veneer panel.

Inlay woods are also used in the art of marquetry. Marquetry is the making of a graphic design, often a floral, using small, individually placed pieces of inlay. Marquetry was especially popular in the William and Mary period at the end of the seventeenth century, and it has been used to some degree ever since.

This floral design is typical of marquetry.

REFINISHING VENEER

Veneer requires some special care if it is to be refinished. Naturally, since it is much thinner than furniture made of solid wood, it is far more fragile. You should never use water while stripping veneer, and be careful when sanding veneer not to use sandpaper that is too coarse or to over-sand the veneer. Doing either of these things will ruin your veneer. Otherwise, refinishing veneered furniture is very similar to refinishing those pieces made of solid wood.

Staining is important to many veneered pieces. An example is a mahogany pedestal table with a pedestal made of poplar. It is important that the poplar be stained properly for appearance's sake. This is an excellent example of when the "natural beauty of the wood" will give the piece a less than professional look.

SUMMARY: VENEER AND INLAYS

- A great look can be achieved using a beautiful veneer wood that would be prohibitively expensive (or impossible) to use as solid wood.

- Veneer styles include Jacobean (oak); William and Mary (marquetry); Chippendale (mahogany); Hepplewhite (Amboyna Burl); and Sheraton (satinwood).

- Veneer can be half-sawn, quarter-sawn, or half-round sliced.

- Veneer can be book matched, slip matched, random matched, or used in a variety of patterns such as diamond, herringbone, and V-shaped.

- Inlays are often geometric patterns.

- Marquetry generally employs a floral design with very small pieces of inlay.

- Veneer must be refinished carefully as its thinness makes it quite fragile.

9.
Furniture Styles

CHIPPENDALE

Thomas Chippendale (1718-79) is probably the best known furniture maker ever. His name serves as a title for much of the English furniture of the mid to late eighteenth century, as well as much American furniture into the early nineteenth century. Chippendale was a talented craftsman, but his great fame comes in large part from his book, *The Gentleman and Cabinet Maker's Director*. In fact, while there is no way to know what Chippendale actually produced, it is known that he was not a carver. All of the decoration that characterizes "Chippendale" furniture was done by workers in his shop. His greatest skill was found in the organization of his shop and the talented artists he employed.

The Chippendale style features elements that recall ancient Greek and Roman architecture, such as columns and capitals in the Classical orders. Several French Rococo motifs appear in this style as well, including scallop shells, "C"- and "S"-shaped scrolls, leaves, and ribbons. Chippendale also used Gothic components such as the quatrefoil. He depicted themes from Aesop's fables in his *Director*, and his style is marked by sumptuous decoration throughout.

American Chippendale furniture is less ostentatious than the original, and introduces aspects of the Queen Anne style already considered out of date in England, such as the claw-and-ball foot. In both the American version and the British original, mahogany was the most widely used cabinet wood. This wood had become so widely available that pieces were made of solid mahogany rather than veneered with mahogany over a less costly wood.

HEPPLEWHITE

Even more than Chippendale, George Hepplewhite (?-1786) owes his fame to books rather than to actual pieces of furniture. Hepplewhite was an obscure London cabinetmaker who collected hundreds of designs for furniture, which his wife compiled after his death into *The Cabinet-Maker and Upholsterer's Guide*. His style was not original, but he did not intend it to be. He merely wanted to bring the neo-classical style of Robert Adam to those outside London and those who could not afford Adam's custom designs.

Besides the many Neo-Classical devices one would expect, Hepplewhite innovated two aspects of design; one seen exclusively in chairs, and the other seen in both chairs and tables. The first of these was the shield-shaped back Hepplewhite designed for chairs. Though this certainly was a new and attractive chair back design, it actually gave little support and is rather fragile. The second feature considered typical of Hepplewhite is the square, tapered, straight leg. Again, while this does give an interesting profile to the furniture, it often puts the entire piece out of proportion.

Decoration was one of the hallmarks of Hepplewhite's style. Ears of corn, "Prince of Wales" feathers, and lavish draperies often appear as carved ornaments. Many pieces were japanned, and there was widespread use of veneer and inlay woods,

Examples of Chippendale style.

especially the extremely rare "Amboyna Burl," veneer cut from the burls of the Narra tree in Borneo.

SHERATON

Thomas Sheraton (1751-1806) is best known as a furniture designer, but he spent much of his life as a writer and an evangelist. His pamphlets on topics of religion and morality appeared before he ever wrote a word regarding furniture. He came to London in about 1790 and published his first and most widely known book, *The Cabinet-Maker and*

Upholsterer's Drawing-Book, in parts from 1791-94. After 1793 in fact, Sheraton did not produce any furniture himself, devoting himself to designs and drawings. He produced *The Cabinet Dictionary* during 1802 and 1803. In the introduction he tried to distance himself from his contemporary Hepplewhite's fantastic designs, saying, "All the designs are capable of being finished exactly as they appear in the engravings."

Sheraton's early designs featured severe, rigidly straight lines and understated decoration, but later in his career he imitated the French Empire style, but poorly, making blocky, cumbersome designs

Examples of Hepplewhite style. Note the characteristic shield back on the chair.

lacking in the genius of his earlier creations. While there were some carved ornaments, more emphasis was placed on marquetry and veneering. Satinwood was the most popular veneer wood, but mahogany remained widespread. Sheraton accented the vertical lines of his pieces, using long, thin legs similar to Hepplewhite's, but while the Hepplewhite leg was rectangular, Sheraton's designs had rounded legs, often turned or vertically fluted. The decorations he chose were from the same Classical vocabulary as Hepplewhite's.

HITCHCOCK

Lambert Hitchcock (?-1852) was a woodworker in Connecticut just after the War of 1812. He was the first mass producer of furniture, putting out about 15,000 chairs per year from his plant in what is now Riverton, Connecticut, and shipping them all over the East Coast. The chairs were designed of interchangeable parts and were shipped in parts so that they could be assembled on site.

Hitchcock chairs are essentially small, open-back side chairs. They were always painted black and had stencils in bronze or other colors on them, in imitation of Oriental lacquerwork.

DUNCAN PHYFE

Duncan Phyfe (1768-1854) was the first well-known American furniture maker. He worked in New York City from about 1795 through 1847. Phyfe employed more than one hundred craftsmen at his peak, and amassed a personal fortune of $500,000 by the time he died in 1854.

Phyfe differs from many of the other designers described here in that he gained fame purely for his handiwork; he never published a book of designs or patterns. He certainly did not have a purely original style. Many of his ideas and devices came from French Directoire and English Regency works. His modifications to common Classical motifs, such as acanthus leaves and carved lyres, became influential in their own right. His approach to the acanthus leaves, called "water leaves" by his contemporar-

ies, simplified each leaf down to a pair of gently undulating grooves bisected by a thin, raised ridge. He also gave new prominence to the lyre, which had been used as a decorative motif by Sheraton and Robert Adam, among others. Phyfe often placed the lyre in the backs of chairs and on the arms of sofas, even using it as the pedestal for a table.

The decoration Phyfe used most often was reeding. His typical design for a chair leg had reeding oriented horizontally at the top and vertical reeding down the length of the leg itself. His reeding is similar to Sheraton's. The aesthetic effect of this reeding was to accent the lines of the piece and the shape made by these lines. Other than reeding, Phyfe had a limited vocabulary of ornamentation, which he repeated for greater visual weight. This vocabulary included bowknots, thunderbolts, wheat, cornucopiae, and draperies with tassels, in addition to the aforementioned acanthus leaves and lyres. On the legs of some of his pieces, Phyfe simulated fur with carving, and he carved paw feet on most of his pieces.

ART DECO

The Art Deco style developed over a period of about fifteen years, from approximately 1910 until 1925, before it came into widespread use. In 1925 an exhibition of decorative arts (*arts decoratifs* in French; hence the name Art Deco) was held in Paris. This exhibition had been planned for 1914, but World War I delayed it. This delay had allowed for the growth of the Art Deco style into full flower before anyone had really taken note of it. The style became popular in America and Europe, but it was always a French style.

Art Deco reacted against the Modernist credo that function should take precedence over beauty. Early Art Deco used many of the same Classical motifs and designs seen to some degree in every style since Chippendale. Egyptian elements were extremely popular, especially because of the discovery of King Tutankhamen's tomb in 1922. As the style developed, it moved away from these Classical themes and began using Modernist elements that became more typical of pure Art Deco.

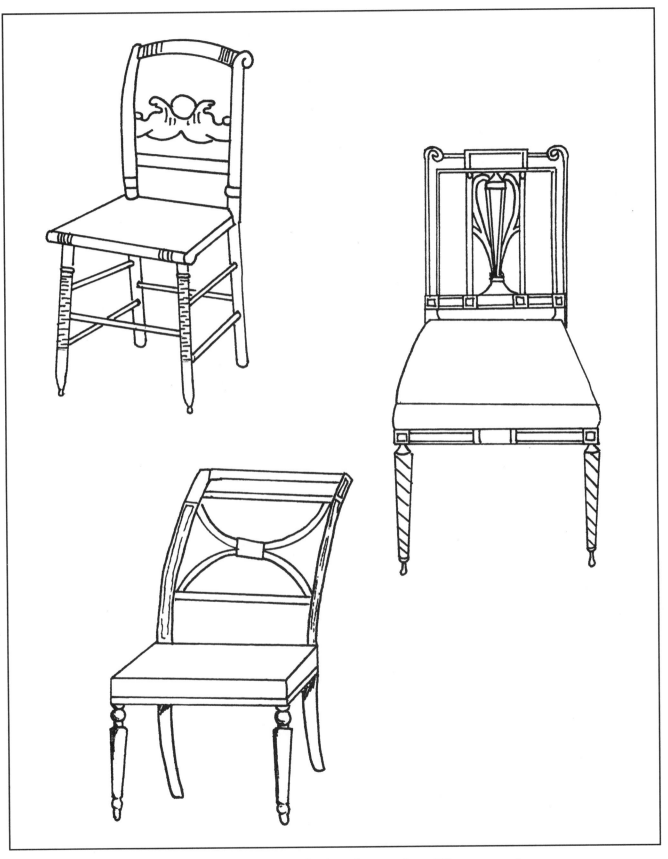

A Hitchcock chair (upper left) and examples of Sheraton style.

Examples of Duncan Phyfe's style. The lyre was a motif he used frequently.

The Art Deco craftsman had to know the preceding style of decorative arts, Art Nouveau, which featured many geometric figures, as well as aspects of several styles of the early 1900s, including Cubism and Fauvism. From Fauvism came bright, hot colors, and from Cubism came the ability to see the piece as the sum of its parts as well as a whole. The machine age also gave Art Deco several other devices. Common decorations included inscribed radio waves, lightning bolts, and electrical currents.

One of the hallmarks of the Art Deco style was an interest in making the piece look unique in design, but especially so in appearance. Many kinds of coverings were used as a top coat for furniture. Exotic veneers, including amboyna, Macassar ebony, and zebrawood, were inlaid with everything from mother-of-pearl to ivory. Gilding was used widely, and furniture was covered with snakeskin, sharkskin (called shagreen), tortoiseshell, and leather. If simple lacquer was applied, it was sprayed and worked to a high gloss. New materials, especially non-organic materials, were very popular. Glass and metal were used as never before. In fact, by the end of the 1920s, metal had almost completely superseded wood as a furniture material.

EMPIRE

The Empire style originated in France with the rise of Napoleon. It hearkened even further back than any previous style, looking not only to Classical Greece and Rome, but further still to the Egypt of the pharaohs. Empire furniture has a distinctly sculptural feel, with broad, sweeping curves. The feeling engendered by the furniture marks its break from the Federal style, which was more understated and esoteric. One of the problems with the Empire style is that less well-designed pieces can seem clunky, heavy, and mechanical.

Technology brought about several artistic innovations in this period. The introduction of a circular veneer saw that could slice veneer ten strips to the inch (as opposed to seven strips per inch) made possible the veneering of curved surfaces. In addition, the thinner strips of veneer cost less, so exotic woods such as zebrawood and rosewood came within the reach of more people. Also, the use of the steam-driven lathe made turning of legs far easier and far more common than ever before.

The other advance in technology had nothing to do with furniture; it had to do with furniture finishes. Looking for a briefer, less expensive process than the typical four coats of varnish, cabinetmakers adopted the French polish process at this time. The only thing I can add to what I said earlier about French polish is that the French, oddly enough, call it "English polish."

Typical pieces of the Empire period in America were as varied as the fancy chairs of Lambert Hitchcock and the fastidious copies of the ancient Greek *klismos* and Roman *curule* chairs. This era also saw the sofa become common for the first time. Sofas had previously been available only to the richest members of American society. There were several popular styles, most with some link to the Greeks or Romans. The most common and least expensive, honestly titled "the plain sofa," took its form from a Roman sofa called a *fulcra*. The slightly more expensive "box sofa" had a more substantial profile and gave a more self-contained feel. The most expensive sofa at this time was the Grecian couch, whose form was related to the Ottoman benches without arms made at this time. Ottomans were often used as window seats.

Another innovation of the Empire period was the center table, which was to become today's coffee table. These tables had heavy pedestals for bases, ending in heavy paw feet. The most popular table of this era, however, was the pier table (low table, often with a mirror).

Two more new arrivals in the American home in the Empire period were the pianoforte and the sideboard. All of these new types of furniture, as well as the appearance of pieces previously reserved for the very rich, show the happy coincidence of technology with the burgeoning economy after the end of the War of 1812.

Examples of Empire style.

FEDERAL

As the name suggests, Federal furniture is American furniture from the period after the formation of the federal government in 1789. Since England was still culturally prevalent in the new nation, this style consists of American furniture makers giving their interpretations of the English styles that had preceded the Revolution. The roots of this style lie with architect and designer Robert Adam. Adam returned to England after a five-year trip to Italy fascinated by the Classical Greek and Roman designs he had seen. He spent the rest of his career bringing designs like those he had seen to the wealthiest people in eighteenth-century England.

The Federal style copied Classical works less slavishly than Adam did. Hepplewhite's book was the standard text for furniture in this era, so it's not surprising that the Federal style features more decoration than Adam's unadorned designs. The American Federal style strikes a balance between the rococo elements of Chippendale's work and the simplicity of Adam's neo-Classicism. The tapered Hepplewhite leg predominates, and devices typical of Hepplewhite and Chippendale are common, with one significant addition. In honor of the new nation, eagles appear all over furniture of this era. Inlays and veneers are common.

QUEEN ANNE

Although named for the English queen who reigned from 1702 until 1714, this style became popular in the United States between 1730 and 1760. The greatest innovation of the Queen Anne style was the cabriole leg, replacing the straight leg of the William and Mary style. Often a scallop shell was carved on the knee, and the foot was either split into three separate points (called a *trifid*) or raised slightly off the ground on a pad.

The gentle curve of the cabriole leg recurred throughout the Queen Anne style. Designers aspired to the Classical "line of grace" or "line of beauty" (essentially an "S" curve). This curve gives the furniture a solid simplicity without making it look blocky and stolid. The carved shell motif was basically the only ornamental carving seen in Queen Anne furniture. The main outlet for the artist came in veneering. Walnut was the most popular wood for veneering, holding a position similar to that of mahogany in the Chippendale period. Japanning was widely used to finish pieces of this period.

Cultural developments introduced new pieces of furniture in this era. England made peace with France in 1713, ending a costly, lengthy war, and as more people made more money, the market for furniture grew. This was an era of specialized furniture, marking the first widespread use of such pieces as the tea table and the card table.

REGENCY

The name "Regency" refers to a very specific period of time when George, Prince of Wales (later George IV), became Prince Regent in 1811, taking control of Britain from his unstable father, George III. The artistic exemplar of the Regency style was architect Thomas Hope. Hope had spent eight years on his grand tour, traveling throughout southern Europe and visiting Egypt, Turkey, and Sicily. Hope published his theories of design in a book, as did most other influential designers, and his work was titled *Household Furniture and Interior Decoration*.

Hope's ideas and motifs shared some common ground with the French Empire style that had developed slightly earlier. Both went to Egypt, as well as Greece and Rome, for their inspiration. Chairs were based on original models found in Pompeii, and sofas found their roots in the daybeds and couches of Rome. Two of the leaders of the French Empire school, Charles Percier and Pierre Fontaine, had also practiced as architects, and their works, much as Hope's pieces in Great Britain, have an architectural look to them. This architectural aspect is most clearly seen in bookcases, which had facades that closely followed the temple fronts of Rome.

The English Regency produced furniture of a massive quality or of delicate weight, while French

Empire furniture kept a middle road between these two extremes. The sphinx commonly seen in France is replaced in England by the panther, gryphon, or lion; in addition, English household furniture featured the "Trafalgar" leg, similar to the sabre leg of Duncan Phyfe. English pieces of this era featured fine, delicate craftsmanship, focusing on the lines of the piece as a whole, not concerning themselves with overly intricate carvings.

SHAKER

The Shakers were a Christian religious sect centered in New England and New York in the late eighteenth and early nineteenth centuries. Mother Ann Lee, the founder of the sect, described the responsibility of the Believer (as Shakers called themselves) thus: "To labor to make the way of God your own; let it be your inheritance, your treasure, your occupation, your daily calling." Taking that attitude, one can see how seriously the Shaker craftsman took their work. Their goal was perfection, for their work was not for their use but for God's. They produced extremely simple designs, free of ornament, which were suited to specific functions. Therein lies the Shakers' innovation. Their first concern was not appearance but utility. Typical Shaker furniture is constructed of solid pine or maple, with no veneer or decoration, although some pieces, especially built-in pieces such as cupboards and day beds, were painted a light blue.

VICTORIAN

The Victorian era takes its name, as do so many furniture styles, from the reigning English monarch. Queen Victoria (1819-1901; reign 1837-1901) held the longest reign of any British ruler. This period was marked by a series of revivals of earlier styles, although without reaching back into antiquity. First, the Victorians went to the Middle Ages, rediscovering the Gothic style, and later they found the rococo style of Louis XIV and Louis XV. The last stage of the Victorian revivals featured a new interpretation of the Classical Greek, Roman, and Egyptian styles, which had first been used by Chippendale.

The Victorian era saw the use of furniture as a status symbol. With the rise of industrialization, the structural and decorative elements of woodworking became increasingly less expensive. Basically, it became difficult to tell a $2 chair from a $50 one. In an effort to show their high social position relative to their neighbors, people had to somehow make their furniture stand out, and the most common way to do this was upholstery. Common woods could be stained to mirror exotic ones, but sumptuous fabric in elaborate patterns was hard to copy. Use of these fabrics clearly differentiated expensive furniture from that covered with the most common upholstery of the time, black horsehair. Many pieces in the Victorian era were upholstered to the point that the frame of the piece could not be seen at all.

The early Victorian period, from 1830 to 1850, saw the rise of the Gothic revival. It was more than aesthetic taste that led to this revival. Many felt that Classical motifs of the previous periods, from Adam through Empire, smacked of a pagan, irreligious society. The Gothic era, a time of little domestic architecture and art, was a natural era to find appropriately reverent devices. The two styles differed in everything down to their lines. The lines of the Classical artist were horizontal and gentle, while the Gothic craftsman used sharply curved vertically oriented lines. (The inherent message was that the lines aimed — as people should — to heaven.)

The decorations used by the Gothic revivalist included the rose window, the quatrefoil, and tracery. The basic structure remained much the same as it had in the Empire style.

The Gothic style had a wider audience in England than in America. The English were reviving a style they had seen the first time around, but it was entirely new to America. In America the most common use of Gothic pieces was by churches and universities. It was considered too pretentious a style for widespread use in the average household, in addition to being too expensive for most people to acquire more than a few pieces. When it did appear in domestic furniture, it was generally limited to one or two rooms, most commonly the sitting room and the library.

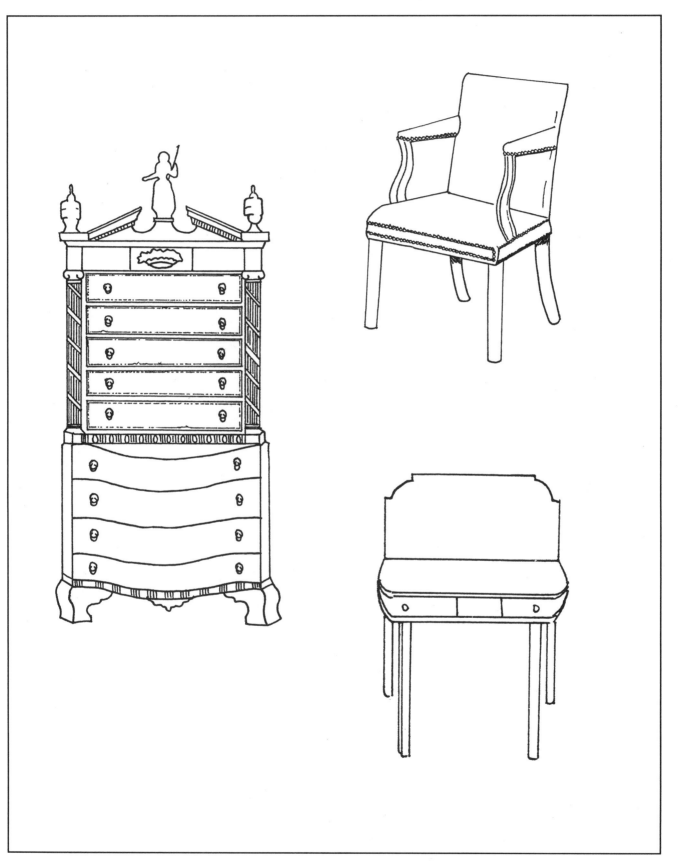

Examples of Federal style.

Examples of Queen Anne style.

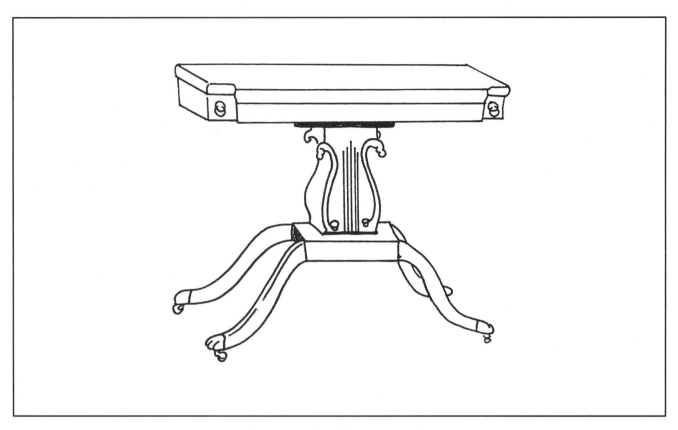

An example of Regency style.

In the middle Victorian period, from 1850 to 1870, the Rococo revival took precedence. This was an adaptation of the French Rococo rather than a strict re-creation, and was more popular for both aesthetic and financial reasons than Gothic works. This era saw the development of the parlor as the most important room of the house. Here guests were received and entertained, and the family made their status clear through their parlor furniture. Overstuffed sofas predominated, and entertainment was provided by the family piano or the melodeon, a cheaper type of organ.

The bedroom took the second most important station in the Victorian household. The basic Victorian bedroom suite included a carved bedstead, a chest of drawers, a washstand, and a dresser. The wardrobe, popular in other eras, was made obsolete by the rise of the built-in closet. The bedstead featured a high headboard and low footboard and lacked bed hangings, which were no longer necessary for warmth because of the development of central heating.

The Renaissance revival was the last of the Victorian revivals, lasting from approximately 1860 to 1880. This period went through three phases, the first of which looked back to the style of Louis XIV, France's "Sun King." This was followed by a renewal of the designs of Louis XVI, and the last stage, called neo-Grec, used elements from ancient Greece, Rome, and Egypt. An individual piece could include facets from each of these three phases. The Renaissance revival is best considered a composite style. The designers of the Renaissance revival period did not copy earlier designs so much as they made unique, updated interpretations of them.

Artisans such as Leon Marcotte used the surface of the furniture much as a painter uses a canvas. This painterly approach was exemplified by the use of inlays and line designs cut into the surface of the wood and filled with gold leaf. Designers also used burled wood panels and ebonized wood to give the surface greater decorative effect. This developed from the cabinetwork of the Louis XIV period, and another French innovation brought back in the

Examples of Shaker style.

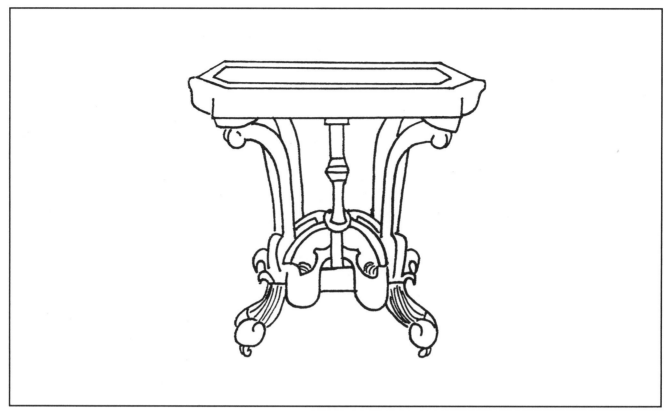

Example of Victorian style.

Renaissance revival was the placement of mounts and sculptural plaques against flat surfaces, such as the sides of pedestals. These pieces were then offset by inlaid exotic woods or ebonized woods.

The neo-Grec revival brought back such elements as the broken pediments and arched pediments of the Greeks, and produced pieces with an angular profile and a segmented surface with many broken lines. Smaller elements such as balustered legs with Classical capitals were also reprised. This revival did not feature much carving. The two-dimensionality cited above was also seen in neo-Grec designs. Inlays and veneers are commonly used.

The dining room gained prominence in the Renaissance revival. The drop-leaf table was replaced by tables with a central pedestal base. The bedroom changed slightly, too. The bed grew larger in the Renaissance revival, until it nearly overpowered the rest of the furniture.

Popular motifs of the Victorian era included naturalistic carving featuring birds, roses, grapes, and vines. The cabriole leg returned to prominence, and the "C" and "S" scrolls last seen in Chippendale were used for further decoration and for structural members such as legs and arms of chairs. Two aspects of the typical Victorian chair are the balloon back and overstuffed upholstery. This upholstery suggests one of the watchwords of the Victorian era: comfort.

Another trend of the Victorian designer was the desire to innovate by using new materials. This led to the use of cast iron, wire, and even papier-mâché in furniture design. At the same time, furniture constructed from organic substances became popular. Wicker and bamboo furniture are examples that combine the desire for new materials with the wish to use purely organic objects. Rustic furniture took the organic approach to an extreme. Cabinetmakers used the shapes found in nature, putting branches

Examples of Victorian style.

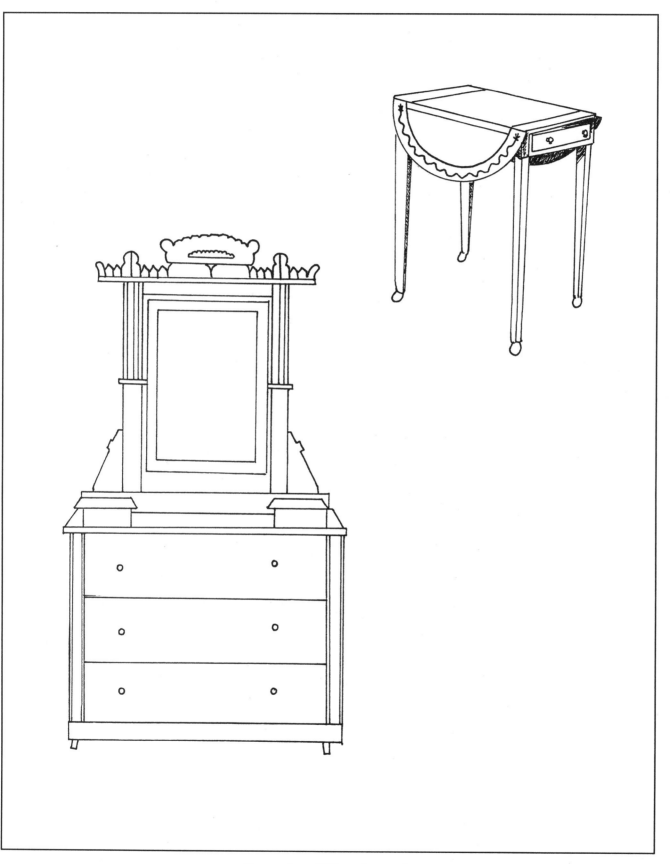

Examples of Victorian style.

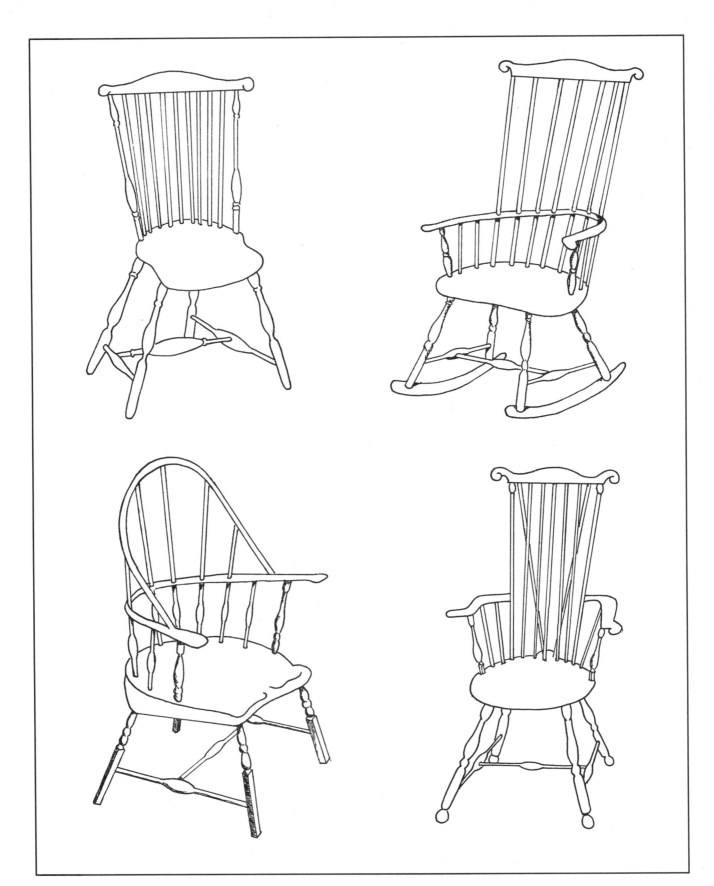

Windsor chairs.

into furniture without processing them except for stripping off the leaves. Also, as the Western frontier gained myth-like status, chairs were made entirely from horns, literally incorporating the animals of the Great Plains into the drawing rooms of the East Coast.

WINDSOR CHAIRS

The Windsor chair is one of the most popular American furniture forms. First popular in England in the 1720s, they became far more common in America after the Revolutionary War. These chairs were originally made from pliable green wood left when woodlands were cut back to protect farmland. Since they were produced from what would otherwise have been waste, Windsor chairs were inexpensive, even though the process was quite intricate. Windsor chair makers would produce a large number of one part at a time, assembling the chairs as required. The hoop back of the Windsor chair consisted of only one piece of wood, often steamed to increase its flexibility. This wood was then put in a frame and allowed to dry in a rounded shape. This border was then drilled and placed over the spindles which were drilled into the seat.

SUMMARY: FURNITURE STYLES	
Style	**Characteristics**
Chippendale	Greek and Roman architectural features
	scallop shells, scrolls, leaves, ribbons
	mahogany
American Chippendale	claw-and-ball foot
	mahogany
Hepplewhite	shield-back chairs
	square, tapered, straight leg
	ears of corn, feathers, draperies
	japanning, use of veneer and inlay woods, especially Amboyna Burl
Sheraton	straight lines, understated decoration
	marquetry, veneering
	rounded legs, turned or fluted
	satinwood, mahogany
Hitchcock	mass-produced chairs
	open-back side chairs, black, with stencils in bronze or other colors

SUMMARY: FURNITURE STYLES	
Style	**Characteristics**
Duncan Phyfe	lyres, acanthus leaves, reeding
	bowknots, thunderbolts, wheat, cornucopiae
	paw feet
Art Deco	geometric designs
	radio waves, lightning bolts, electrical currents
	exotic veneers: Amboyna, zebrawood, Macassar ebony
	gilding, snakeskin, sharkskin, tortoiseshell, leather
	glossy lacquer finishes
	glass and metal
Empire	Classical Greek, Roman, and Egyptian themes
	veneering of curved surfaces
	zebrawood, rosewood
	French polish
American Empire	sofa, Ottoman bench
	center table, pianoforte, sideboard
Federal	influence of Robert Adam
	Classical Greek and Roman designs
	eagles
	veneers and inlays
Queen Anne	cabriole leg, carved shell motif
	walnut veneer, japanning
	tea table, card table
Regency	Egyptian, Greek, and Roman inspiration
	architectural look, especially in bookcases
	panther, gryphon, lion
	"Trafalgar" leg

SUMMARY: FURNITURE STYLES	
Style	**Characteristics**
Shaker	simple design
	functional simplicity
	pine, maple
	no veneer or decoration
Victorian	revival of earlier styles
	furniture as status symbol
	emphasis on upholstery
Gothic revival	sharply curved, vertically oriented lines
Rococo revival	overstuffed sofas, bedstead with high headboard, low footboard, no hangings
Renaissance revival	painterly approach
	inlays, line designs with gold leaf
	exotic or ebonized woods
Other features typical of Victorian style	naturalistic carving — birds, roses, grapes, vines
	scrollwork
	balloon back chairs
	cast iron, wire, papier-mâché furniture
	wicker, bamboo

Conclusion

How do you determine whether the piece you want restored should be refinished or not? I often think of an old jalopy sitting in a field. Is it worth more in its present condition or after restoration? You must ask yourself, "Will refinishing devalue my piece of furniture?" This question is most often asked of me when I'm in the basement or garage, looking at a piece that is not being used because it is in such bad shape. As the owner of the piece, the final decision as to what to do to the piece is yours. You may have to rely on the advice of a craftsman or other person who knows furniture to help you make a decision, regardless of who does the work.

Working on furniture started as a hobby for me and turned into a business. I am thankful to be in business, doing something I enjoy. At times, I have to admit it has been stressful turning a hobby into a business but I can't imagine that I could enjoy doing anything else.

I learned that the time I was willing to give to the community writing columns, holding seminars, teaching classes, or just taking the time to answer a question on the phone has all been returned to me threefold. By reading my book and gaining some information about finishes and refinishing, you will be able to help a friend or a loved one add care and value to his or her furniture and cabinets.

Glossary

ANTIQUE — The current cut-off date for antique furniture is approximately a hundred years. For appraisal purposes, the federal government considers any piece dating from before 1930 to be antique.

BENTWOOD — Bentwood furniture is made from wood that has been bent into a permanent shape by heat, moisture, and pressure. Famous makers of bentwood furniture include John H. Belter and Thonet.

BLUSHING — A finish that is "blushing" has a white ring in it, resulting from the condensation and slow evaporation of water from the surface of the finish.

BURL — Abnormal growths on the trunks and branches of trees. Often cut into veneer strips, burls have unique mottled figures.

CARNAUBA — A type of wax secreted by a species of palm tree. This is one of the hardest, and therefore best, waxes available. It is so hard that it must be combined with a softer wax, such as beeswax, to make it spreadable. The higher the percentage of carnauba in your furniture wax, the better the wax.

CLEAR FINISHES — Clear finishes are those that leave a transparent film on the surface of the wood. This group includes lacquer, shellac, and polyurethane.

CROTCH VENEER — Crotch veneer is taken from places where tree branches meet the trunk. It has V-shaped figures, which look beautiful when matched.

DOVETAIL JOINT — A joint made from interlocking tenons, which resemble a bird's tail feathers.

ENAMEL — A paint, varnish, etc., that is dried to a hard, glossy finish.

EPOXY — Epoxy is a resinous adhesive. When the epoxy resin is combined with an aqueous solution and mixed thoroughly, it forms an extremely strong bond.

FIGURE — Figure refers to the pattern found in a piece of wood.

FRENCH POLISH — French polishing, also called French finishing, is the process of giving a high gloss finish by padding on several thin layers of shellac.

GLAZING — Glazing is the application of a thin wash coat over the finish coat, which is then wiped off. This tempers the shade of the finish coat, giving it a flatter sheen. Glazing is often used as a way of aging a piece of furniture.

GRAIN — The grain of a piece of wood is the orientation of its fibers. It is very important always to work with the grain; that is, in the same direction as the grain.

GRAINING — Graining is a type of custom painting in which the painter attempts to duplicate the natural grain of wood with paint.

HARDWARE — Hardware includes all parts that are not structural members of a piece of furniture. These include hinges, door knobs, drawer pulls, etc.

INLAY — Inlay is the art of making designs by contrasting the grain, texture, figure, and color of wood, metal, or other materials. Small pieces of these other materials are laid flush with the surface of the wood. Inlay woods are generally veneer woods.

JACOBEAN — Jacobean furniture dates from the reign of James I of England (1603-25) through the reign of Charles II of England (1685-88). The reign of James marked the beginning of continental influence on English furniture, first from France and then stronger influences from Holland. Most Jacobean furniture has a rectilinear outline, with turning used widely. Low-relief carving, in conjunction with inlays, marquetry, and inscibed designs, is a common ornamental effect.

JAPANNING — Japanning is a coating of colored varnish used as a finish coat. It began as an imitation of Oriental lacquerwork, which first came into Europe in the early seventeenth century. It was extremely popular until the mid-eighteenth century.

JOINERY — Joinery is essentially the craft of furniture construction. It does not include design.

LACQUER — Lacquer is the most popular furniture finish of the twentieth century. It consists of resins (derived from nitrocellulose) in solvents.

LAMINATE—Laminating is the process of gluing several thin strips of wood together for increased strength.

LINSEED OIL — Linseed oil is collected from the seeds of the flax plant. Both raw linseed oil and boiled linseed oil are available commercially, but boiled linseed oil is the one used in furniture products.

MARQUETRY — The art of marquetry involves the use of inlays and veneers to make patterns. One of the most common designs made using marquetry is a flower.

MILK PAINT — Milk paint was the typical finish applied in colonial America. Natural pigments (blood, clay, etc.) were used to give the paint color.

This is one of the toughest finishes to remove, but you may not want to as doing so could compromise the historical value of the piece.

MISSION FURNITURE — Mission furniture is a style of furniture based on the Spanish missions of the Southwest. It was part of the Arts and Crafts movement of the early 1900s.

MOLDING — A molding is an applied piece of wood used to define an open space on a piece of furniture. Many moldings for furniture are similar to achitectural elements, such as pediments and cornices.

MORTISE AND TENON — The mortise and tenon is one of the most common joints in furniture making. The mortise is a cavity into which the tenon, a carved part projecting from the end of a piece of wood, fits.

OPAQUE FINISHES — Opaque finishes are those that conceal the wood beneath them. These include paint, japan, and colored lacquer.

ORDERS — The orders of Classical architecture are the different types of columns and capitals, and the arrangement of elements specific to each. The three most commonly seen in furniture are the Doric, the Ionic, and the Corinthian.

PARQUETRY — Parquetry is marquetry in the shape of a geometric figure.

PATINA — A patina on a piece of furniture is the particular color and appearance its finish has taken on with age.

PEDIMENT — The pediment is the triangular piece at the top of the facade of a Classical temple. Pediments are often seen in larger Neo-Classical pieces, such as wardrobes and bookcases.

PICKLED FINISH — Pickled finish gives a dusky patina in contrast with a glossy finish. It is most often used with large-pored woods, such as oak and chestnut.

REPRODUCTION — A reproduction is a copy of a piece of period furniture produced many years after the style in which it was made popular.

SEALER — Sealer, often called sanding sealer, is applied after wood has been stained but before the finish is applied, in order to prevent the stain from leaching through the finish.

SHELLAC — Shellac is a substance secreted by a species of beetle in India. After being processed, it can be dissolved in alcohol and applied as a furniture finish. The material used for French finish is shellac.

SPINDLES — Spindles are the thin vertical pieces that form the back for Windsor chairs, among other pieces of furniture.

SPLAT — The splat is the center piece in the back of a chair frame. These are not seen in chairs with spindled or upholstered backs.

SPREADER — A spreader is a piece put between the legs of a chair to prevent the legs from warping inward.

STAIN — Stain is any product designed to change the natural color of a piece of wood without obscuring the grain.

TRACERY — Tracery is the use of thin bands of wood to make ornamental designs of interwoven, sinuous lines. Tracery first appeared in the Gothic period and is often seen in conjunction with other Gothic elements.

TUNG OIL — Tung oil, also called china nut oil, is an oil finish that dries far faster than linseed oil.

TURNING — Turning is the art of shaping wood into curved forms and cutting ornamental designs in the wood while it turns on a lathe.

VARNISH — Varnish is a finish consisting of resin suspended in a solvent. The first varnishes were oil varnishes, which used oil as a solvent. Current varnishes are called spirit varnishes because they use mineral spirits as a solvent.

VENEER — Veneer is wood cut into very thin strips, which is used as a top layer on furniture. Often, exotic woods are used as veneer to give greater beauty to a piece of furniture.

WARP — A warped piece of wood is one that has become bent or twisted. This can occur in the curing process or may occur due to uneven pressure placed on the wood.

Appendices

1.
Magazines

American Woodworker
33 East Minor Street
Emmaus PA 18098
(800) 666-3111

Fine Woodworking
Taunton Press
63 South Main Street
P.O. Box 5506
Newtown CT 06470-9971
(203) 426-8171

Popular Woodworking
1320 Galaxy Way
Concord CA 94520

Shop Notes
2200 Grand Avenue
Des Moines IA 50312
(800) 333-5854

Today's Woodworker
P.O. Box 6782
Syracuse NY 13217-9916

Wood
P.O. Box 55050
Boulder CO 80322-5050
(800) 374-9663

Woodshop News
35 Pratt Street
Essex CT 06426

Woodsmith
2200 Grand Avenue
Des Moines IA 50312
(800) 333-5075

Woodwork
Ross Periodicals, Inc.
33 Redwood Drive
P.O. Box 1529
Ross CA 94957
(415) 382-0580

Woodworker's Business News
5604 Alameda Place NE
Albuquerque NM 87113
(800) 645-9292

Woodworker's Journal
P.O. Box 1629
New Milford CT 06776
(203) 355-2694

2.
Books

Bell, J. Munro, *The Furniture Designs of Chippendale, Hepplewhite, and Sheraton*. Robert M. McBride & Co., 1938.

Davis, Kenneth, and Thom Henvey, *Restoring Furniture*. New York: Arco Publishing Company, Inc., 1978.

Edlin, Herbert L., *What Wood is That?*. New York: Viking Penguin, Inc., 1969

Fine Woodworking (Editorial Staff), *Fine Woodworking on Finishing and Refinishing*. Newtown, CT: The Taunton Press, 1986.

Fine Woodworking (Editorial Staff), *Finishes and Finishing Techniques*. Newtown, CT: The Taunton Press, 1991.

Grotz, George, *The Furniture Doctor*. New York: Doubleday, 1983.

Hall, Alan, and James Heard, *Wood Finishing and Refinishing*. New York: Holt, Rinehard and Winston, 1981.

Higgins, Alfred, *Common-Sense Guide to Refinishing Antiques*. New York: Funk & Wagnalls, 1976.

Jackson, Albert, and David Day, *Good Wood Handbook*. White Hall, VA: Betterway Publications, 1991.

Kassay, John, *The Book of Shaker Furniture*. Amherst, MA: The University of Massachusetts, 1980.

Lamb, George N. *The Mahogany Book*. Chicago: Mahogany Association, Inc., 1943.

Margon, Lester, *Construction of American Furniture Treasures*. New York: The Home Craftsman Publishing Corporation, 1949.

Naeve, Milo N., *Identifying American Furniture*. Nashville, TN: American Association for State and Local History, 1989.

Savage, Jessie D., *Professional Furniture Refinishing for the Amateur*. New York: Harper & Row, 1974.

3.
Wood Types and Qualities

SOFTWOODS		
Type	**Color**	**Finish Quality**
California redwood	red/brown	good
Cedar of Lebanon	light brown	good
Douglas fir	red/brown	fair
Eastern white pine	light yellow	good
European redwood	red/brown	good
Larch	red/brown	fair
Norway spruce	light yellow	good
Ponderosa pine	light yellow	fair
Silver fir	light yellow	good
Sitka spruce	reddish white	good
Southern longleaf pine	reddish yellow	very good
Sugar pine	light yellow	fair
Western hemlock	light brown	good
Western red cedar	red/brown	good
Western white pine	light yellow	good
Yellow cedar	yellow	good
Yew	reddish	good

HARDWOODS		
Type	**Color**	**Finish Quality**
Basswood	whitish	good
Beech	red/brown	good
Black walnut	dark brown	very good
Boxwood	yellow	good
Brazilwood	red/brown	good
Bubinga	red/brown	good
Butternut	brown	good
Cherry	red/brown	very good
Cocobolo	black	very good
European ash	light brown	good
European chestnut	light brown	good
European oak	light brown	good
European sycamore	whitish yellow	good
Hickory	red/brown	good
Lignum vitae	red/brown	good
Purpleheart	purple/brown	very good
Red oak	whitish brown	very good
Rock maple	whitish	good
Satinwood	gold/brown	good
Silver maple	whitish	good
Sycamore	whitish brown	good
Tulipwood	red/brown	good
White ash	whitish	good
White elm	whitish	good
White oak	light brown	very good
Yellow birch	yellow	good
Yellow poplar	yellow/green	good
Zebrawood	reddish black	good

4.
Wood Descriptions

ALDER — This lightweight hardwood resists denting and abrasion. It is a pale pinkish brown to whitish. The grain is uniform and alder takes a stain well. *Alnus rubra.*

ASH — This wood is strong, hard, and long-lasting. Creamy white to dark reddish brown. Its strong grain resembles that of oak. It is often used for its strength, especially in bentwood furniture. *Fraxinus americana.*

BASSWOOD — Basswood is used for its ability to take on stains that enable it to masquerade as other woods. It is normally a creamy brown to creamy white and is often used for furniture legs. It is sometimes referred to as "linden." *Tilia americana.*

BEECH — This wood is strong, hard, and dense. White or slightly reddish, its texture is like that of maple, and it is often mistaken for maple. It bends well and is often used for turning. *Fagus granifolia.*

BIRCH — Birch is strong, heavy, and hard. It is creamy to reddish brown and can be stained to appear like cherry, mahogany, or walnut. *Betula alleghaniensis.*

CHERRY — Cherry is durable, strong, and moderately hard. It is light to dark reddish brown, carves well, and polishes beautifully. *Prunus serotina.*

CHESTNUT — This wood is uncommon because of the blight that affects it. It is reddish brown. Victorian furniture makers often used it to imitate walnut or oak. *Castanea dentata.*

ELM — Elm is medium heavy and hard. It is light to dark brown and sometimes has red tints. It is often used for veneer. *Ulmus americana.*

GUM — Gum is medium-hard, heavy, and strong. This reddish brown wood is used as veneer, carves well, and can simulate walnut or mahogany. *Liquidambar styraciflua.*

MAHOGANY — This hard, heavy, strong wood is yellow-tan, brown, or brown-red. It has a lovely texture and finishes smooth with a high luster. There are several types: Cuban (*Swietenia mahogani*), Honduras (*Swietenia macrophylla*), and African (*Khaya ivorensis*).

MAPLE — Maple is strong, heavy, and hard. It is off-white to a light reddish brown. Its figures include blister, curly, fiddleback, and bird's eye. *Acer saccharum.*

OAK — Oak is strong and hard. It is generally whitish to light reddish brown. *Quercus alba* (American white oak); *Quercus borealis* (red oak).

PINE — This is a light, solid wood generally found in off-white to pale reddish brown tones. *Pinus monticola.*

POPLAR — This wood is medium to light weight and moderately soft. Generally yellow to yellowish brown, it is useful for simulating other woods. *Liriodendron tulipifera.*

ROSEWOOD — Rosewood is durable and hard. It has a wide color range: browns, brown-black, purplish. It was extensively used in veneers and inlays in the eighteenth century. *Dahlbergia nigra* (Brazilian); *Dahlbergia latifolia* (East Indian).

TEAK — Teak is durable and heavy, generally yellow to dark brown. It is found in some carved furniture (especially Oriental pieces) and modern pieces. *Tectona grandis.*

WALNUT — This wood is heavy, strong, and hard. It is light to dark chocolate brown. It takes a finish well. Used as a veneer and furniture wood. European walnut has a lighter color. *Juglans nigra* (American walnut); *Juglans hindsii* (California walnut); *Juglans regia* (European walnut).

5.
Wood Joints

WOOD JOINTS	
Corner Joints	**Comments**
Butt	weak joint in all materials
Dovetail	strong decorative joint, good for all softwoods and hardwoods
Dowel	stronger than butt joint, good for most woods
Miter	fairly strong joint, best with softwoods
Rabbet	fairly strong joint, good for softwoods and hardwoods
Edge Joints	**Comments**
Biscuit	strongest edge joint, works well with almost all woods
Butt	simplest edge joint, moderate strength, useful for all softwoods, some hardwoods
Dowel	strong edge joint, for all softwoods and hardwoods
Shiplap	strong edge joint, for all softwoods and hardwoods
Tongue and Groove	strong edge joint, for all softwoods and hardwoods
T-Joints	**Comments**
Biscuit	strong joint for all softwoods and hardwoods
Butt	very weak joint, must be reinforced
Dado	strong joint, good for all softwoods and hardwoods
Dovetail	very strong joint, for all softwoods and hardwoods

6.
Problem-Solver's Guide

PROBLEM	MATERIALS NEEDED	TECHNIQUE
Dirty finish; appears to need refinishing	Superfine steel wool Hand cleaner Clean cloth	Apply hand cleaner to steel wool; rub gently to remove dirt. Buff with cloth.
Finish needs cleaning, waxing	Superfine steel wool Paste wax Clean cloth	Apply wax to piece with steel wool, using moderate pressure. Buff with cloth.
Dull shellac finish	Denatured alcohol Clean cloth	Put small amount of denatured alcohol on cloth. Rub quickly across finish.
Dull finish (1)	Minwax stain Clean cloths	Mix stain as directed. Apply with clean cloth. Wipe off excess with second cloth.
Dull finish (2)	220 grit sandpaper Bartley gel stain 2-inch sponge brush Clean cloth	Sand lightly to smooth and remove any loose finish. Dip tip of sponge brush in stain, brush on with grain. Wipe off excess immediately.
New finish needed over old finish (1)	Hand cleaner 220 grit sandpaper Denatured alcohol White shellac 3-inch sponge brush	Clean old finish with hand cleaner. Sand lightly. Thin shellac as necessary with denatured alcohol. Brush on shellac with sponge brush in thin, even coat.
New finish needed over old finish (2)	Hand cleaner 220 grit sandpaper Bartley gel finish 3-inch sponge brush Clean cloth	Clean old finish. Sand lightly. Brush on Bartley gel finish with grain, wiping off excess immediately.
Rubmarks (1)	Hand cleaner Superfine steel wool Clean cloth	Apply hand cleaner to steel wool, rub with grain. Buff with cloth.

PROBLEM	MATERIALS NEEDED	TECHNIQUE
Rubmarks (2)	Hand cleaner Superfine steel wool Clean cloths Artist's brush Minwax stain	Apply hand cleaner to steel wool, rub with grain. Buff with clean cloth. Apply stain with artist's brush. Wipe off gently with cloth.
Rubbed-through edges (1)	Permanent felt marker matching finish color	Lightly run marker over worn edge.
Rubbed-through edges (2)	Minwax stain Artist's brush	Use artist's brush dipped in stain to cover worn edge.
Nicks and scratches	Minwax stain Clean cloths Razor blade Artist's brush	Put stain on cloth and wipe on piece. Remove specks of paint with razor blade. Use artist's brush dipped in stain for any remaining small spots.
Scratch — minor	Water or vegetable oil Rottenstone Clean cloth Paste wax	Dampen cloth with water or vegetable oil. Sprinkle rottenstone over scratch. Rub with cloth in circular motion. Paste wax for sheen.
Scratch — medium serious	600 grit wet/dry sandpaper Small sponge Vegetable oil or water Rottenstone Clean cloth Paste wax	Cut sandpaper in strips so each piece is 1/2 inch wider than sponge. Apply 1 tablespoon oil or water to scratch. Sand over scratch but not through finish. Wax for sheen.
Scratch — deep		Burn-in needed for deep scratch. Do not attempt without experience.
Cigarette burn	Pocket knife Artist's brush Varnish-based sanding sealer 600 grit wet/dry sandpaper Bartley gel finish	Scrape away burned finish with pocket knife. Use artist's brush to apply sanding sealer — several coats with drying time between. Sand to level. Finish with Bartley gel finish.

PROBLEM	MATERIALS NEEDED	TECHNIQUE
Clouds in finish (1)	Hand cleaner Superfine steel wool Clean cloth Paste wax	Clean with hand cleaner and steel wool. Wipe with cloth. Wax using steel wool with paste wax.
Clouds in finish (2)	Mineral oil Cotton swab	Put two or three drops of oil on cotton swab. Work into finish in small circle over spot.
Press marks	Paste wax Steel wool	Apply paste wax to steel wool and rub area gently.
Dents (1)	Water Needle Iron	Apply small amount of water to dent. May use needle to press holes into center of dent. Allow water to penetrate several minutes. Heat area with top of iron; do not allow iron to touch the wood.
Dents (2)	Water Cloth Iron	Place cloth on piece and dampen over dent. Iron over cloth. NOTE: Be careful with veneered pieces; veneer could lift.
Gouges	220 grit sandpaper Wood filler Putty knife	Sand lightly. Apply wood filler with putty knife.
Stains	Two-part wood bleach Brush Hair dryer	Mix wood bleach as directed, apply to stained area with brush. Use hair dryer to activate bleach.
Cabinets — soft finish	Varnish-based sanding sealer Polyurethane Hand cleaner 220 grit sandpaper 3-inch sponge brush Pieces of toweling	Clean with hand cleaner on toweling. Sand lightly. Apply sanding sealer to soft area and let dry. Sand lightly and apply polyurethane.

Index

About the Author

Brad Hughes has twenty-two years of hands-on experience in refinishing furniture and has owned a furniture restoration business for eleven years. He has written a newspaper column on furniture care for three years, and teaches classes and seminars on the subject. His current labor of love is restoring the furniture at Ash Lawn-Highland, the home of President James Monroe.

A complete catalog of Betterway Books is available FREE by writing to the address shown below, or by calling toll-free 1-800-289-0963. To order additional copies of this book, include $3.00 postage and handling for one book, and $1.00 for each additional book. Ohio residents add 5½% sales tax. Allow 30 days for delivery.

Betterway Books
1507 Dana Avenue
Cincinnati, Ohio 45207

Stock is limited on some titles; prices subject to change without notice.